I0438602

Prepared in cooperation with the Centers for Disease Control and Prevention

Occurrence of Selected Pharmaceutical and Organic Wastewater Compounds in Effluent and Water Samples from Municipal Wastewater and Drinking-Water Treatment Facilities in the Tar and Cape Fear River Basins, North Carolina, 2003–2005

Open-File Report 2009–1046

U.S. Department of the Interior
U.S. Geological Survey

Occurrence of Selected Pharmaceutical and Organic Wastewater Compounds in Effluent and Water Samples from Municipal Wastewater and Drinking-Water Treatment Facilities in the Tar and Cape Fear River Basins, North Carolina, 2003–2005

By G.M. Ferrell

Prepared in cooperation with the Centers for Disease Control and Prevention

Open-File Report 2009–1046

U.S. Department of the Interior
U.S. Geological Survey

U.S. Department of the Interior
KEN SALAZAR, Secretary

U.S. Geological Survey
Suzette M. Kimball, Acting Director

U.S. Geological Survey, Reston, Virginia: 2009

For product and ordering information:
World Wide Web: http://www.usgs.gov/pubprod
Telephone: 1-888-ASK-USGS

For more information on the USGS—the Federal source for science about the Earth, its natural and living resources, natural hazards, and the environment:
World Wide Web: http://www.usgs.gov
Telephone: 1-888-ASK-USGS

Suggested citation:
Ferrell, G.M., 2009, Occurrence of selected pharmaceutical and organic wastewater compounds in effluent and water samples from municipal wastewater and drinking-water treatment facilities in the Tar and Cape Fear River basins, North Carolina, 2003–2005: U.S. Geological Survey Open-File Report 2009–1046, 45 p.

(Available only online at http://pubs.water.usgs.gov/ofr2009-1046)

Contents

Abstract...1

Introduction...1

    Purpose and Scope 1

    Acknowledgments...2

    Study Area...2

    Study Design and Site Selection 2

    Sample Collection and Analysis...7

    Quality Assurance and Quality Control 11

Phase 1 Results..12

Treated Effluent Samples from Wastewater-Treatment Facilities.................................12

Raw Water Samples from Drinking-Water Treatment Facilities.....................................12

Phase 2 Results..22

Effluent Samples Before and After Disinfection at Wastewater-Treatment Facilities.....22

Drinking-Water Samples at Various Stages of Treatment..43

Summary..43

References Cited...44

Figures

1–3.   Maps showing—

      1.   Tar and Cape Fear River basins and physiographic provinces
in North Carolina...2

      2.   Sampling sites, wastewater-treatment plant outfalls, water-supply intakes,
major streams, and municipalities in the Tar River basin, North Carolina..........3

      3.   Sampling sites, wastewater-treatment plant outfalls, water-supply intakes,
major streams, and municipalities in the Cape Fear River basin,
North Carolina 4

Tables

1.   Sampling locations at selected municipal wastewater-treatment facilities in
the Tar and Cape Fear River basins, North Carolina, 2003 and 2005....................5

2.   Sampling locations at selected municipal drinking-water treatment facilities
in the Tar and Cape Fear River basins, North Carolina, 2003 and 2005...............6

3.   Pharmaceutical compounds and metabolites analyzed in effluent and water samples
from municipal wastewater- and drinking-water treatment facilities in the Tar and
Cape Fear River basins, North Carolina, 2003 and 2005..8

4.   Organic wastewater compounds analyzed in effluent and water samples from
municipal wastewater- and drinking-water treatment facilities in the Tar River and
Cape Fear River basins, North Carolina, 2003 and 2005..9

5. Antibiotics, antibiotic metabolites, and pharmaceutical compounds analyzed in effluent and water samples from municipal wastewater- and drinking-water treatment facilities in the Tar and Cape Fear River basins, North Carolina, February–August 2005 11

6. Concentrations of selected pharmaceutical compounds in samples of treated effluent from municipal wastewater-treatment facilities in the Tar and Cape Fear River basins, North Carolina, September 2003 13

7. Concentrations of selected organic wastewater compounds in treated effluent from municipal wastewater-treatment facilities in the Tar River Basin, North Carolina, September 2003 14

8. Concentrations of selected organic wastewater compounds in treated effluent from municipal wastewater-treatment facilities in the Cape Fear River Basin, North Carolina, September 2003 16

9. Concentrations of selected pharmaceutical compounds in raw water from municipal drinking-water treatment facilities in the Tar and Cape Fear River basins, North Carolina, August–September 2003 18

10. Concentrations of selected organic wastewater compounds in raw water samples from municipal drinking-water treatment facilities in the Tar River basin, North Carolina, September 2003 19

11. Concentrations of selected organic wastewater compounds in raw water samples from municipal drinking-water treatment facilities in the Cape Fear River basin, North Carolina, August–September 2003 21

12. Concentrations of selected pharmaceutical compounds and metabolites in effluent from municipal wastewater-treatment facilities, before and after disinfection, in the Tar and Cape Fear River basins, North Carolina, May–July 2005 23

13. Concentrations of selected organic wastewater compounds and dissolved organic carbon in effluent from municipal wastewater-treatment facilities, before and after disinfection, in the Tar and Cape Fear River basins, North Carolina, May–July 2005.....24

14. Concentrations of selected antibiotics, antibiotic metabolites, and pharmaceutical compounds in effluent from municipal wastewater-treatment facilities, before and after disinfection, in the Tar and Cape Fear River basins, North Carolina, May–July 2005..27

15. Concentrations of selected pharmaceutical compounds and metabolites in water samples at various stages of treatment from municipal drinking-water treatment facilities in the Tar River Basin, North Carolina, February and July 2005 29

16. Concentrations of selected pharmaceutical compounds and metabolites in water samples at various stages of treatment from municipal drinking-water treatment facilities in the Cape Fear River basin, North Carolina, July–August 2005 30

17. Concentrations of selected organic wastewater compounds in water at various stages of treatment from municipal drinking-water treatment facilities in the Tar River basin, North Carolina, February and July 2005 32

18. Concentrations of selected organic wastewater compounds in samples of water at various stages of treatment from municipal drinking-water treatment facilities in the Cape Fear River basin, North Carolina, July and August 2005 35

19. Concentrations of selected antibiotics, antibiotic metabolites, and pharmaceutical compounds in water at various stages of treatment from municipal drinking-water treatment facilities in the Tar River Basin, North Carolina, February and June 2005 40

20. Concentrations of selected antibiotics, antibiotic metabolites, and pharmaceutical compounds in water at various stages of treatment from municipal drinking-water treatment facilities in the Cape Fear River Basin, North Carolina, February and June 2005...41

Conversion Factors

Multiply	By	To obtain
mile (mi)	1.609	kilometer (km)
square mile (mi^2)	2.590	square kilometer (km^2)
million gallons per day (Mgal/d)	0.04381	cubic meter per second (m^3/s)

Horizontal coordinate information is referenced to the North American Datum of 1983 (NAD 83).

Concentrations of chemical constituents in water are given in micrograms per liter (μg/L) unless otherwise noted.

Occurrence of Selected Pharmaceutical and Organic Wastewater Compounds in Effluent and Water Samples from Municipal Wastewater and Drinking-Water Treatment Facilities in the Tar and Cape Fear River Basins, North Carolina, 2003–2005

By G.M. Ferrell

Abstract

Samples of treated effluent and treated and untreated water were collected at 20 municipal wastewater and drinking-water treatment facilities in the Tar and Cape Fear River basins of North Carolina during 2003 and 2005. The samples were analyzed for a variety of prescription and nonprescription pharmaceutical compounds and a suite of organic compounds considered indicative of wastewater. Concentrations of these compounds generally were less than or near the detection limits of the analytical methods used during this investigation. None of these compounds were detected at concentrations that exceeded drinking-water standards established by the U.S. Environmental Protection Agency. Bromoform, a disinfection byproduct, was the only compound detected at a concentration that exceeded regulatory guidelines. The concentration of bromoform in one finished drinking-water sample, 26 micrograms per liter, exceeded North Carolina water-quality criteria. Drinking-water treatment practices were effective at removing many of the compounds detected in untreated water. Disinfection processes used in wastewater treatment—chlorination or irradiation with ultraviolet light—did not seem to substantially degrade the organic compounds evaluated during this study.

Introduction

Numerous studies have shown the widespread occurrence of pharmaceutical compounds, organic wastewater compounds (OWCs), and antibiotics in surface waters (Aherne and Briggs, 1989; Daughton and Ternes, 1999; Hirsch and others, 1999; Kolpin and others, 2002). Removal of organic compounds by conventional wastewater- and water-treatment practices primarily occurs by microbial degradation and adsorption to particulate matter followed by removal of the particulate matter by processes such as settling, flocculation, and filtration.

Many organic compounds are degraded during disinfection as a result of oxidative reactions that occur when wastewater or water is treated with chlorine (either free chlorine or chloramine) or ozone (Jones and others, 2005; Watkinson and others, 2007). Ultraviolet (UV) irradiation, commonly used to disinfect wastewater, can facilitate degradation of some organic compounds. Incomplete removal by conventional wastewater-treatment processes results in the discharge of some of these compounds in municipal wastewater effluent. Incomplete removal and recalcitrance to natural degradation have contributed to the presence of these compounds in surface waters at locations downstream from wastewater-treatment plant (WWTP) outfalls. Several studies have shown that pharmaceutical compounds, OWCs, and antibiotics are present in the raw (untreated) water used by municipal drinking-water facilities, and some compounds (for example, carbamazepine) are not degraded by chlorination (Clara and others, 2004; Vieno and others, 2007). Concerns about possible human health effects of these compounds in surface waters used for drinking-water supply have lead to studies of the effects of water-treatment processes on removal of these compounds (Ternes and others, 2002; Stackelberg and others, 2004 and 2007; Westerhoff and others, 2005). The ecological and human health effects associated with exposure to low concentrations of these compounds in drinking water are not well known (Jones and others 2004), and consequently, few regulatory standards have been established for pharmaceutical compounds (Falconer, and others, 2006; Fent and others, 2006).

Purpose and Scope

The purpose of this report is to present the results of a study, conducted by the U.S. Geological Survey in cooperation with the Centers for Disease Control and Prevention, to characterize the occurrence of pharmaceutical compounds and OWCs in municipal drinking-water supplies at water-treatment facilities in the Tar and Cape Fear River basins. The occurrence of pharmaceutical compounds and OWCs in treated effluent from municipal WWTPs upstream from the drinking-water supply intakes also was evaluated. Samples were obtained in 2003 and 2005 at times of low streamflow.

Acknowledgments

This study was funded by the Centers for Disease Control and Prevention. The assistance and information provided by managers, operators, and laboratory personnel at wastewater- and water-treatment facilities in the Tar and Cape Fear River basins are greatly appreciated.

Study Area

Sampling was conducted to assess the occurrence of pharmaceutical compounds, OWCs, and antibiotics in drinking-water supplies obtained from streams in the Tar and Cape Fear River basins (fig. 1). The Cape Fear River basin is the largest river basin in North Carolina and is heavily urbanized in its headwaters where the cities of High Point, Greensboro, Burlington, Durham, and Raleigh are located. In contrast, the headwaters of the Tar River basin are largely rural. The Tar and Cape Fear Rivers originate in the Piedmont Physiographic Province, flow through the Coastal Plain, and ultimately terminate at the Atlantic Ocean or, in the case of the Tar River, the Pamlico Sound (fig. 1). Characteristics of both rivers change along this route, with a general decrease in

velocity and increases in depth and dissolved organic carbon concentrations.

Study Design and Site Selection

To facilitate selection of sites for sample collection, locations of municipal WWTP outfalls and drinking-water treatment plant (DWTP) intakes were obtained from records of the North Carolina Department of Environment and Natural Resources (North Carolina Department of Environment and Natural Resources, 2004 and 2006) and are shown in figures 2 and 3 for the Tar and Cape Fear River basins, respectively. The WWTP and DWTP locations, as well as information provided in water-supply plans (North Carolina Department of Environment and Natural Resources, 2002) were used in the selection of sampling sites. Information about the WWTPs and DWTPs sampled during this study is provided in tables 1 and 2, respectively. Because policies of the U.S. Geological Survey prohibit the public release of information pertaining to the location and ownership of municipal WWTPs and DWTPs (Katherine Lins, U.S. Geological Survey, Office of Water Information, written commun., July, 17, 2008), only generalized site locations are shown for water-supply intakes and WWTP outfalls, and the facilities at which samples were collected are referred to by site identifiers rather than facility names.

The first phase of sampling was designed to characterize major sources of pharmaceutical compounds and OWCs upstream from drinking-water intakes. To accomplish this, samples of treated effluent were collected in August and September 2003 from outfalls at 10 municipal

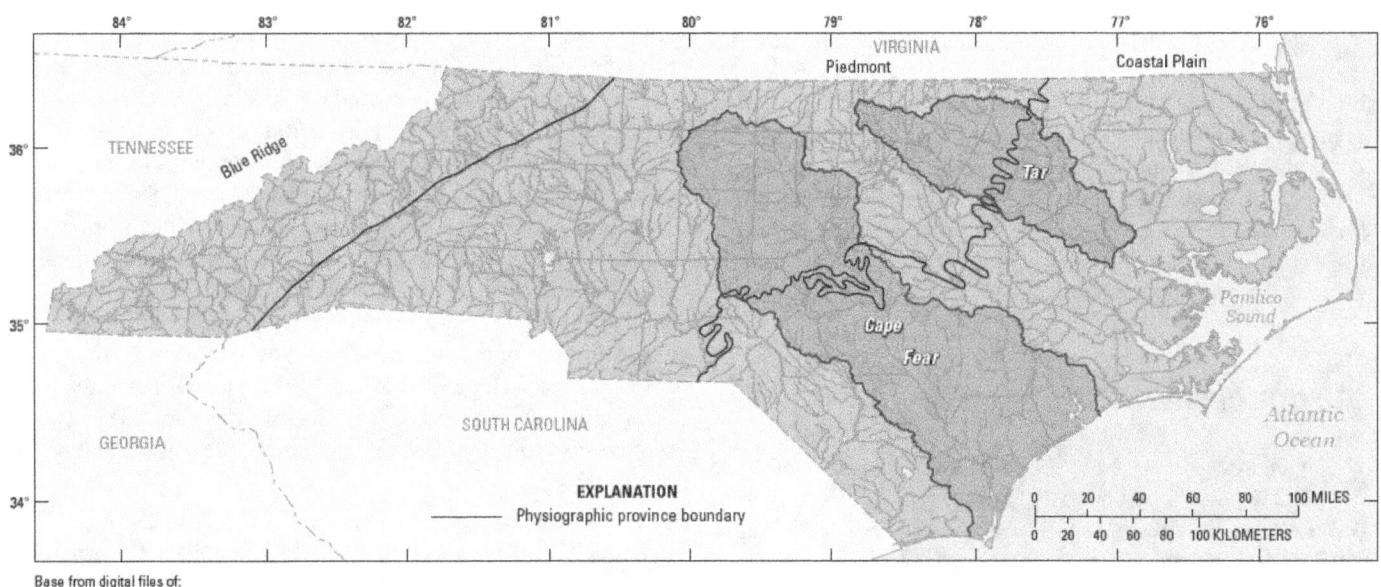

Base from digital files of:
U.S. Department of Commerce, Bureau of Census,
  1990 Precensus TIGER/Line Files-Political boundaries, 1991
U.S. Environmental Protection Agency, River File 3
U.S. Geological Survey, 1:100,000 scale

Figure 1. Tar and Cape Fear River basins and physiographic provinces in North Carolina.

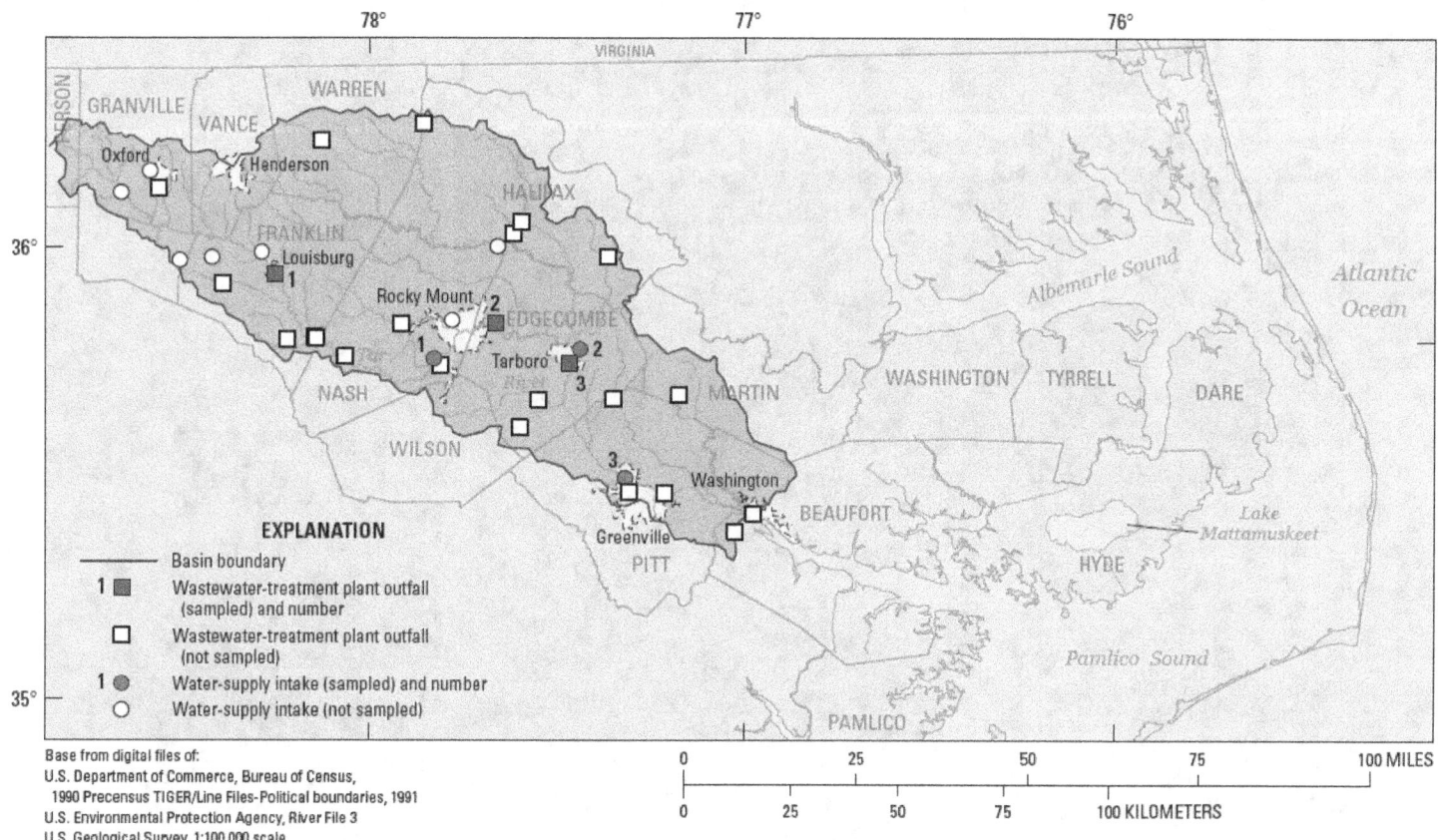

Figure 2. Sampling sites, wastewater-treatment plant outfalls, water-supply intakes, major streams, and municipalities in the Tar River basin, North Carolina.

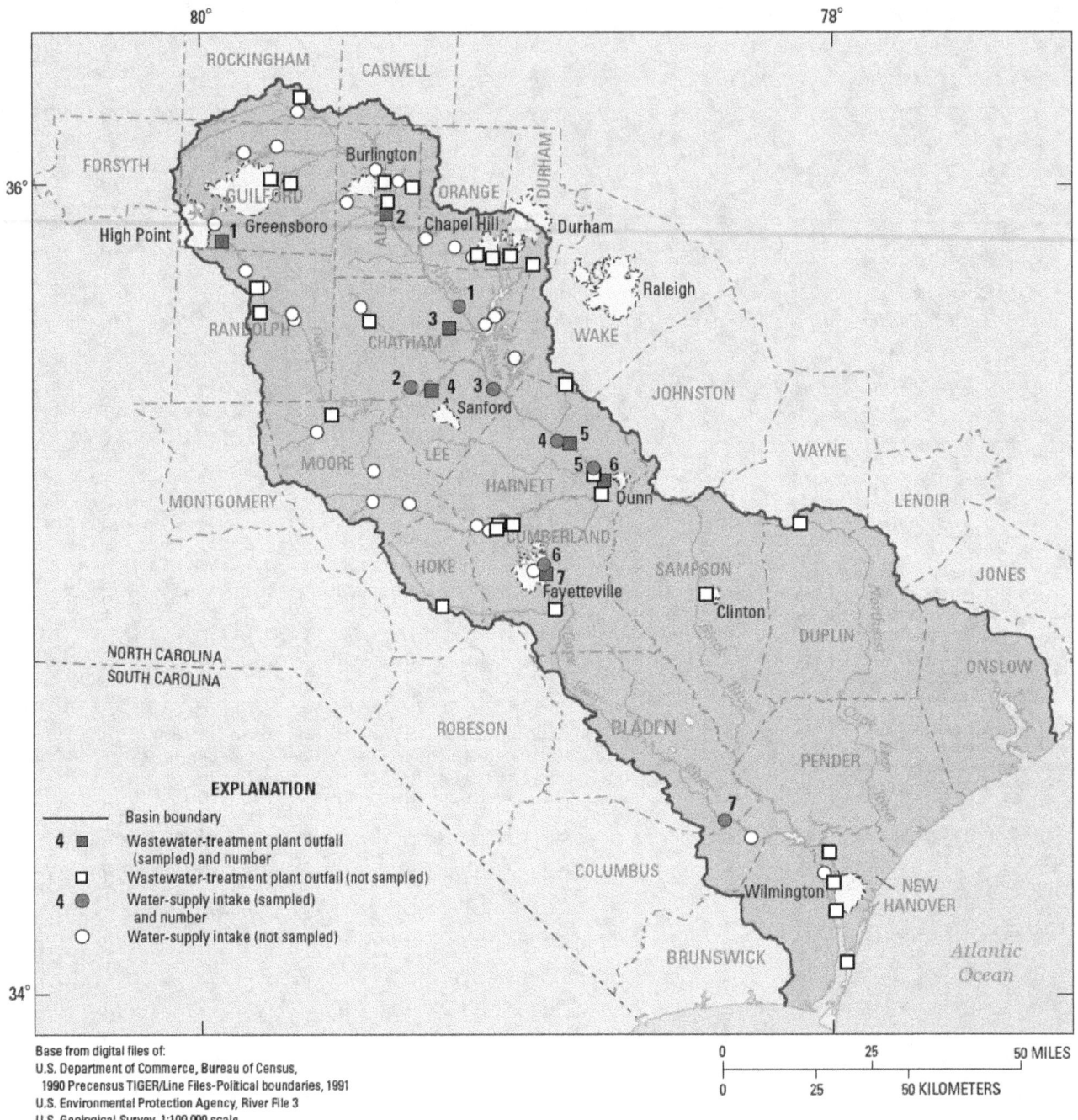

Figure 3.   Sampling sites, wastewater-treatment plant outfalls, water-supply intakes, major streams, and municipalities in the Cape Fear River basin, North Carolina.

Table 1. Sampling locations at selected municipal wastewater-treatment facilities in the Tar and Cape Fear River basins, North Carolina, 2003 and 2005.

[Mgal/d, million gallons per day; UV, ultraviolet]

Map number	Site identifier	Sample type (disinfection status)	Sample-collection date(s)	Disinfection process	Receiving water	Permitted capacity (Mgal/d)[a]
Figure 2			Tar River basin			
1	Tar-WW01	treated effluent (after UV disinfection)	09/11/2003 and 05/06/2005	UV irradiation	Tar River	1.37
		treated effluent (before UV disinfection)	06/06/2005			
2	Tar-WW02	treated effluent (after chlorination)	09/05/2003	chlorination	Tar River	21.0
3	Tar-WW03	treated effluent (after chlorination)	09/05/2003 and 07/22/2005	chlorination	Tar River	5.0
		treated effluent (before chlorination)	07/22/2005			
Figure 3			Cape Fear River basin			
1	CF-WW01	treated effluent (after chlorination)	09/13/2003	chlorination	Richland Creek (tributary of Deep River)	16.0
2	CF-WW02	treated effluent (after chlorination)	09/13/2003	chlorination	Alamance Creek (tributary of Haw River)	12.0
3	CF-WW03	treated effluent (after UV disinfection)	09/09/2003 and 08/04/2005	UV irradiation	Roberson Creek	0.75
		treated effluent (before UV disinfection)	08/04/2005			
4	CF-WW04	treated effluent (after chlorination)	09/10/2003	chlorination	Deep River	12.0
5	CF-WW05	treated effluent (after chlorination)	09/10/2003	chlorination	Cape Fear River	0.75
6	CF-WW06	treated effluent (after chlorination)	09/09/2003	chlorination	Juniper Creek (tributary of Cape Fear River)	3.75
7	CF-WW07	treated effluent (after chlorination)	09/09/2003 and 07/14/2005	chlorination	Cape Fear River	25.0
		treated effluent (before chlorination)	07/14/2005			

[a] Source of data: North Carolina Department of Environment and Natural Resources (2002).

Table 2. Sampling locations at selected municipal drinking-water treatment facilities in the Tar and Cape Fear River basins, North Carolina, 2003 and 2005.

[mi², square mile; Mgal/d, million gallons per day; WWTP, wastewater-treatment plant]

Map number	Site identifier	Sample type (disinfection)	Sample-collection date(s)	Primary source of water	Drainage area at intake (mi²)	County	Year round population served[a,b]	Permitted capacity (Mgal/d)[b]	Number of upstream WWTP outfalls
Tar River basin									
1	Tar-DW01	raw water	09/05/2003	Tar River	780	Nash	68,400	25.0	7
2	Tar-DW02	raw water settled water finished water (chlorination)	09/5/2003 and 02/11/2005 02/11/2005 02/11/2005	Tar River	2,180	Edgecombe	11,100	6.0	13
3	Tar-DW03	raw water impounded settled (ozonation) filtered clearwell finished water (chlorination)	09/5/2003 and 07/12/2005 07/12/2005 07/12/2005 07/12/2005 07/12/2005 07/12/2005	Tar River	2,650	Pitt	73,000	22.5	18
Cape Fear River basin									
1	CF-DW01	raw water	09/09/2003	Haw River	1,270	Chatham	2,400	1.5	7
2	CF-DW02	raw water finished water (chlorination)	9/9/2003 and 8/4/2005 08/04/2005	Deep River	1,060	Chatham	1,200	0.5	4
3	CF-DW03	raw water	09/10/2003	Cape Fear River	3,210	Lee	34,600	12.0	16
4	CF-DW04	raw water	09/09/2003	Cape Fear River	3,460	Harnett	78,000	18.0	17
5	CF-DW05	raw water	09/10/2003	Cape Fear River	3,750	Harnett	9,930	8.0	18
6	CF-DW06	raw water impounded settled clearwell finished water (chlorination)	9/10/2003 and 07/14/2005 07/14/2005 07/14/2005 07/14/2005 07/14/2005	Cape Fear River	4,350	Cumberland	178,000	32.0	25
7	CF-DW07	raw water preozonation settled-second time clarified and prefiltration (ozonation) finished (chlorination)	08/28/2003 and 07/21/2005 07/21/2005 07/21/2005 07/21/2005 07/21/2005	Cape Fear River	5,250	New Hanover	102,000	25.0	27

a Population served does not include sales.

b Source of data: North Carolina Department of Environment and Natural Resources (2002).

WWTPs—3 in the Tar River basin and 7 in the Cape Fear River basin. Samples of raw water also were collected at the DWTP that had the nearest intake downstream from each of the sampled WWTP outfalls. The WWTPs and DWTPs at which samples were collected during this investigation are identified in figures 2 and 3 and described in tables 1 and 2. To minimize the effects of dilution, low streamflow conditions were chosen for collection of samples during the initial phase of this study (Kolpin and others, 2004).

The second phase of sampling, which occurred from February to August 2005, addressed the effects of treatment practices on pharmaceutical compounds, OWCs, and antibiotic compounds in wastewater effluent and drinking water. Four WWTPs were selected for sampling of effluent—two in the Tar River basin and two in the Cape Fear River basin. Effluent was sampled before and after disinfection at each of these WWTPs. Disinfection techniques used at these WWTPs were either UV irradiation or chlorination (table 1). Five DWTPs were selected for additional sampling from the 10 plants at which raw water samples had been collected during the first phase of sampling. DWTPs were selected on the basis of treatment practices, with emphasis on use of ozonation, proximity of upstream municipal WWTP outfalls, and occurrence of pharmaceutical compounds and OWCs in the sample collected during the first phase of this investigation. Treatment practices used by the DWTPs vary considerably and range from conventional treatment processes, such as those used at sites Tar-DW02 and CF-DW02, to advanced treatment processes, such as biofiltration using granular activated carbon, at site CF-DW07. Disinfection practices used at the DWTPs selected for sampling during phase 2 included chlorination and ozonation (table 2).

Sample Collection and Analysis

Wastewater samples obtained during the first phase of the study were collected as close as practical to the point where the effluent entered the receiving water body. Wastewater samples obtained during the second phase of the study were collected at points where the effluent entered and exited the chlorination chamber or UV disinfection chamber. Drinking-water samples obtained during the first phase of sampling were of untreated water and were collected from the water intakes. Drinking-water samples collected during the second phase of the study were obtained at various points in the water-treatment process depending on the individual water plant. Samples were collected in polytetrafluoroethylene (PTFE) bottles, filtered through a glass fiber filter using PTFE tubing and either a PTFE or stainless steel filtration unit, and processed onsite. Sampling and filtration equipment were cleaned with methanol and organic-free water between collection of samples. Ascorbic acid was added to chlorinated samples following filtration to quench the oxidative reaction associated with residual chlorine (Mark Sandstrom, U.S. Geological Survey, National Water Quality Laboratory

Methods Research and Development Program, and Greg Delzer, U.S. Geological Survey, South Dakota Water Science Center, written commun., January 24, 2007). Samples were placed on ice following collection and chilled during transport to the analyzing laboratories.

Effluent and water samples were analyzed for a variety of pharmaceuticals and organic compounds considered to be indicators of wastewater. Several pharmaceutical and OWC metabolites were also analyzed. Samples were analyzed for 24 compounds, including 20 commonly used prescription and over-the-counter pharmaceutical compounds and metabolites and 4 antibiotic compounds (table 3). Two of the over-the-counter pharmaceutical compounds—miconazole and thiabendazole—are antifungal compounds and are considered to be antibiotics. These compounds were analyzed by solid-phase extraction and high-performance liquid chromatography/mass spectrometry positive-ion electrospray ionization [HPLC/MS–ESI(+)] as described in Cahill and others (2004). No water-quality standards or criteria have been established for these pharmaceutical compounds, metabolites, and antibiotics.

Samples also were analyzed for a suite of 61 organic compounds considered indicative of wastewater (table 4). These analytes, referred to as organic wastewater compounds (OWCs), are widely used in household, industrial, and agricultural settings and include 7 detergent components and degradates; 4 flame retardants; 9 fragrances and flavorants; 11 polycyclic aromatic hydrocarbons (PAHs), fossil fuel components, and combustion byproducts; 11 pesticides; 3 pharmaceuticals; 4 plasticizers; 3 solvents; 4 biogenic sterols; and 5 miscellaneous antioxidants, disinfectants, and disinfection byproducts (table 4). Water-quality standards and criteria established for these analytes are provided in table 4. The OWCs were analyzed by solid phase extraction (SPE) and gas chromatography/mass spectrometry (GC/MS) following methods described by Zaugg and others (2002).

In addition to the pharmaceutical compounds and OWCs described in the previous paragraphs, samples collected during the second phase of the study (February to August 2005) were analyzed for 24 antibiotic compounds, 6 antibiotic metabolites, and 2 pharmaceutical compounds (table 5). These compounds were analyzed by online SPE and liquid chromatography/tandem mass spectrometry (LC/MS/MS) with electrospray ionization (ESI) using multiple reaction monitoring. Positive-ion mode was used for detection of all analytes except chloramphenicol and ibuprofen, which were analyzed in negative-ion mode. Analytical methods for the antibiotics and degradates are based on methods described in Meyer and others (2007). No water-quality standards or criteria have been established for these antibiotic and pharmaceutical compounds.

Several compounds—azithromycin, caffeine, carbamazepine, cotinine, erythromycin, ibuprofen, sulfamethoxazole, and trimethoprim—were analyzed by more than one method. The analytical method with the lowest reporting limit was considered to be the preferred method and is designated as such in tables 3–5. Samples collected during the second phase

Table 3.   Pharmaceutical compounds and metabolites analyzed in effluent and water samples from municipal wastewater- and drinking-water treatment facilities in the Tar and Cape Fear River basins, North Carolina, 2003 and 2005.

[µg/L, microgram per liter; CASRN, Chemical Abstracts Service Registry Number®; --, not established; analytes with known or suspected hormonal activity are shown in **bold** type; analytical method described in Cahill and others (2004)]

Analyte	Reporting limit (µg/L)	CASRN[a]	Primary use/source
Acetaminophen	0.018	103-90-2	Antipyretic, analgesic
Albuterol	0.0115	18559-94-9	Bronchodilator
Azithromycin[b]	0.0022	83905-01-5	Macrolide antibiotic
Caffeine[c]	0.008	58-08-2	Stimulant
Carbamazepine[b]	0.0054	298-46-4	Antiepileptic, anticonvulsant
Cimetidine	0.0061	51481-61-9	Antacid
Codeine	0.0076	76-57-3	Analgesic
Cotinine[c]	0.0068	486-56-6	Nicotine metabolite
Dehydronifedipine	0.0077	67035-22-7	Nifedipine[d] metabolite
Diltiazem	0.0079	42399-41-7	Antihypertensive
1,7-Dimethylxanthine	0.0722	611-59-6	Caffeine metabolite
Diphenhydramine	0.0074	58-73-1	Antihistamine
Erythromycin[b]	0.0046	114-07-8	Macrolide antibiotic
Fluoxetine	**0.0072**	**54910-89-3**	**Antidepressant**
Furosemide	--	54-31-9	Diuretic
Gemfibrozil	0.0064	25812-30-0	Hypolipidemic
Ibuprofen[b]	0.0208	15687-27-1	Analgesic
Metformin	--	657-24-9	Oral hypoglycemic
Miconazole	0.0088	22916-47-8	Antifungal agent
Ranitidine	0.0064	66357-35-5	Antacid
Sulfamethoxazole[b]	0.0321	723-46-6	Sulfonamide antibiotic
Thiabendazole	0.0054	148-79-8	Antifungal agent
Trimethoprim[b]	0.0063	64-75-5	Antibiotic
Warfarin	0.0059	81-81-2	Anticoagulant

[a] This report contains CAS Registry Numbers®, which is a Registered Trademark of the American Chemical Society. CAS recommends the verification of the CASRNs through CAS Client Services[SM].

[b] Secondary method of analysis for this analyte (see table 5 for preferred method of analysis).

[c] Preferred method of analysis for this analyte (see table 4 for secondary method of analysis).

[d] Nifedipine: antianginal, antihypertensive.

Table 4. Organic wastewater compounds analyzed in effluent and water samples from municipal wastewater- and drinking-water treatment facilities in the Tar and Cape Fear River basins, North Carolina, 2003 and 2005.

[µg/L, microgram per liter; CASRN, Chemical Abstracts Service Registry Number®; MCL, maximum contaminant level; LHA, lifetime health advisory; PAH, polycyclic aromatic hydrocarbon; analytes with known or suspected hormonal activity are shown in **bold type**; --, not established; analytical method described in Zaugg and others (2002)]

Analyte	Reporting limit (µg/L)	CASRN	MCL(LHA)[a] (µg/L)	North Carolina water-quality criterion[b] (µg/L)	Primary use/source
Detergent components and degradates					
4-Cumylphenol	**1**	**599-64-4**	--	--	**Detergent metabolite**
p-Nonylphenol (total)	**1**	**104-40-5**	--	--	**Detergent metabolite**
Nonylphenol diethoxylates (NP2EO)	**5**	--	--	--	**Detergent metabolite**
4-n-Octylphenol	**1**	**1806-26-4**	--	--	**Detergent metabolite**
4-t-Octylphenol	**1**	**140-66-9**	--	--	**Detergent metabolite**
4-t-Octylphenol monoethoxylates (OP1EO)	**1**	--	--	--	**Detergent metabolite**
4-t-Octylphenol diethoxylates (OP2EO)	**1**	--	--	--	**Detergent metabolite**
Flame retardants					
Tributyl phosphate	0.5	126-73-8	--	--	Flame retardant
Tri(2-chloroethyl)phosphate (FYROL CEF)	0.5	115-96-8	--	--	Flame retardant
Tri(dichloroisopropyl)phosphate (FYROL PCF)	0.5	13674-87-8	--	--	Flame retardant
Triphenyl phosphate	0.5	115-86-6	--	--	Flame retardant, plasticizer
Fragrances and flavorants					
Acetophenone	0.5	98-86-2	--	3,500	Fragrance, flavoring, solvent
Benzophenone	**0.5**	**119-61-9**	--	--	**Fragrance fixative, manufacturing**
1,3,4,6,7,8-Hexahydro-4,6,6,7,8,8-hexamethylcyclopenta-γ-2-benzopyran (HHCB)	**0.5**	**1222-05-5**	--	--	**Fragrance**
Indole	0.5	120-72-9	--	--	Fragrance
3-Methyl-1H-indole (skatole)	1	83-34-1	--	--	Fragrance, essential oil, fecal indole
Isoborneol	0.5	124-76-5	--	--	Fragrance, flavoring
Menthol	0.5	89-78-1	--	--	Fragrance, flavoring
Methyl salicylate	0.5	119-36-8	--	--	Fragrance, liniment, flavoring
7-Acetyl-1,1,3,4,4,6-hexamethyl-1,2,3,4-tetrahydro-naphthalene (AHTN)	**0.5**	**21145-77-7**	--	--	**Fragrance**
PAHs, fossil fuel components, and combustion byproducts					
Anthracene	0.5	120-12-7	--	0.05	PAH, wood preservative, insecticide
Anthraquinone	0.5	84-65-1	--	--	Oxidative byproduct of anthracene, pigment, bird repellent, plant compound
p-Cresol	1	106-44-8	--	250	wood preservative, combustion byproduct
Fluoranthene	0.5	206-44-0	--	0.11	PAH
Naphthalene	0.5	91-20-3	(100)	52	PAH, combustion byproduct, moth repellant
1-Methylnaphthalene	0.5	90-12-0	--	--	Fuel component, combustion byproduct
2-Methylnaphthalene	0.5	91-57-6	--	50	Fuel component, combustion byproduct
2,6-Dimethylnaphthalene	0.5	581-42-0	--	--	Fuel component
Phenanthrene	0.5	85-1-8	--	--	PAH, dye and pharmaceutical component
Pyrene	**0.5**	**129-00-0**	--	830	**PAH, combustion byproduct, asphalt**
Benzo[a]pyrene	**0.5**	**50-32-8**	0.2	0.0028[c]	**PAH, combustion byproduct**
Pesticides					
Bromacil	**0.5**	**314-40-9**	(70)	--	**Herbicide**
Carbaryl	1	63-25-2	--	0.67	Insecticide
Carbazole	0.5	86-74-8	--	0.76	Insecticide, manufacturing
Chlorpyrifos	**0.5**	**2921-88-2**	(2)	--	**Insecticide**

Table 4. Organic wastewater compounds analyzed in effluent and water samples from municipal wastewater- and drinking-water treatment facilities in the Tar and Cape Fear River basins, North Carolina, 2003 and 2005.—Continued

[µg/L, microgram per liter; CASRN, Chemical Abstracts Service Registry Number®; MCL, maximum contaminant level; LHA, lifetime health advisory; PAH, polycyclic aromatic hydrocarbon; analytes with known or suspected hormonal activity are shown in **bold type**; --, not established; analytical method described in Zaugg and others (2002)]

Analyte	Reporting limit (µg/L)	CASRN	MCL(LHA)[a] (µg/L)	North Carolina water-quality criterion[b] (µg/L)	Primary use/source
Pharmaceuticals					
Diazinon	**0.5**	**333-41-5**	(1)	0.17	**Insecticide**
d-Dichlorvos	1	62-73-7	--	0.12	**Insecticide**
d-Limonene	0.5	5989-27-5	--	--	Fungicide, manufacturing
Metalaxyl	0.5	57837-19-1	--	--	Fungicide
Metolachlor	0.5	51218-45-2	(700)	4,000	Herbicide
Pentachlorophenol	2	**87-86-5**	1	0.27	**insecticide, fungicide, wood preservative**
Prometon	0.5	1610-18-0	(100)	--	Herbicide
Caffeine[d]	0.5	58-08-2	--	--	Stimulant
Cotinine[d]	1	486-56-6	--	--	Nicotine metabolite
Isoquinoline	0.5	119-65-3	--	--	medicinal product, rubber additive, dye
Plasticizers					
Bisphenol A	**1**	**80-05-7**	--	--	**Plasticizer, antioxidant**
Camphor	0.5	76-22-2	--	--	plasticizer, moth repellent, preservative
Triethyl citrate (ethyl citrate)	0.5	77-93-0	--	--	plasticizer, cosmetics, food additive
Tri(2-butoxyethyl) phosphate	0.5	78-51-3	--	--	Plasticizer
Solvents					
Isophorone	0.5	78-59-1	(100)	35	Solvent
Isopropylbenzene (cumene)	0.5	98-82-8	200[e]	320	Solvent, fuel component
Tetrachloroethylene (PCE)	0.5	127-18-4	5(10)	0.7	Solvent, degreaser
Biogenic sterols					
Cholesterol	2	57-88-5	--	--	Plant/animal sterol
3-β-Coprostanol	2	360-68-9	--	--	Fecal sterol (carnivore)
β-Sitosterol	**2**	**83-46-5**	--	--	**Phytosterol**
β-Stigmastanol	2	19466-47-8	--	--	Phytosterol
Miscellaneous compounds					
3-t-Butyl-4-hydroxyanisole (BHA)	5	25013-16-5	--	--	**Antioxidant, food preservative**
1,4-Dichlorobenzene	**0.5**	106-46-7	75(75)	63	**Deodorizer, disinfectant**
5-Methyl-1H-benzotriazole	2	136-85-6	--	--	Antioxidant in antifreeze, anticorrosive
Bromoform	0.5	75-25-2	80[f]	4.3	Chlorination byproduct
Triclosan	1	**3380-34-5**	--	--	**Antimicrobial disinfectant**

[a] MCL and LHA are human health standards or advisories established by the U.S. Environmental Protection Agency (2006). The MCL is the maximum permissible amount of a contaminant in drinking water. MCLs are enforceable for public drinking-water supplies. The LHA is maximum concentration in water of a contaminant that is considered to have no adverse health effects over a lifetime exposure. The LHA is not an enforceable standard. MCLs and LHAs are available online at *http //www.epa.gov/waterscience/criteria/drinking/dwstandards.pdf* (accessed September 15, 2008).

[b] North Carolina water-quality criterion is the more stringent of the water supply, human health, saltwater aquatic life, or freshwater aquatic life criterion listed in North Carolina and U.S. Environmental Protection Agency criteria table (North Carolina Department of Environment and Natural Resources, 2008) available online at *http //h2o.enr.state.nc.us/csu/documents/NC_EPA_Standards_CriteriaTables1-10-08.pdf* (accessed August 15, 2008).

[c] Criterion established for total PAH concentration (applicable to PAHs with demonstrated carcinogenicity).

[d] Secondary method of analysis for this analyte (see table 3 for preferred method of analysis).

[e] Drinking-water equivalent level.

[f] Standard applicable to total trihalomethane concentration.

Table 5.   Antibiotics, antibiotic metabolites, and pharmaceutical compounds analyzed in effluent and water samples from municipal wastewater- and drinking-water treatment facilities in the Tar and Cape Fear River basins, North Carolina, February–August 2005.

[μg/L, microgram per liter; CASRN, Chemical Abstracts Service Registry Number®; --, not applicable; NA, not available; analytical method is described in Meyer and others (2007)]

Analyte	Reporting limit (μg/L)	CASRN	Category	Primary use
Azithromycin[a]	0.005	83905-01-5	macrolide antibiotic	Human
Erythromycin[a]	0.008	114-07-8	macrolide antibiotic	Human/Veterinary
Erythromycin-H_2O (anhydroerythromycin)	0.008	114-07-8	erythromycin metabolite	--
Roxithromycin	0.005	80214-83-1	macrolide antibiotic	Human
Tylosin	0.005	1401-69-0	macrolide antibiotic	Veterinary
Virginiamycin	0.005	8065-94-9	macrolide antibiotic	Veterinary
Ciprofloxacin	0.005	85721-33-1	fluoroquinolone antibiotic	Human/Veterinary
Enrofloxacin	0.005	93106-60-6	fluoroquinolone antibiotic	Veterinary
Lomefloxacin	0.005	98079-51-7	fluoroquinolone antibiotic	Human
Norfloxacin	0.005	70458-96-7	fluoroquinolone antibiotic	Human/Veterinary
Ofloxacin	0.005	82419-36-1	fluoroquinolone antibiotic	Human/Veterinary
Sarafloxacin	0.005	98105-99-8	fluoroquinolone antibiotic	Aquaculture/Veterinary
Sulfadiazine	0.005	68-35-9	sulfonamide antibiotic	Human/Veterinary
Sulfadimethoxine	0.005	122-11-2	sulfonamide antibiotic	Aquaculture/Veterinary
Sulfamethazine	0.005	57-68-1	sulfonamide antibiotic	Veterinary
Sulfamethoxazole[a]	0.005	723-46-6	sulfonamide antibiotic	Human
Sulfathiazole	0.020	72-14-0	sulfonamide antibiotic	Veterinary
Chlortetracycline	0.010	57-62-5	tetracycline antibiotic	Veterinary
Epi-chlortetracycline	0.010	514-53-4	chlortetracycline metabolite	--
Epi-iso-chlortetracycline	0.010	NA	chlortetracycline metabolite	--
Iso-chlortetracycline	0.010	514-53-4	chlortetracycline metabolite	--
Doxycycline	0.010	564-25-0	tetracycline antibiotic	Human/Veterinary
Oxytetracycline	0.010	79-57-2	tetracycline antibiotic	Aquaculture/Beekeeping/ Veterinary
Epi-oxytetracycline	0.010	35259-39-3	oxytetracycline metabolite	--
Tetracycline	0.010	738-70-50	tetracycline antibiotic	Human/Veterinary
Epi-tetracycline	0.010	23313-80-6	tetracycline metabolite	--
Lincomycin	0.005	154-21-2	lincosamide antibiotic	Veterinary
Chloramphenicol	0.010	56-75-7	bacteriostatic antibiotic	Human/Veterinary
Ormetoprim	0.005	6981-18-6	diaminopyrimidine antibiotic	Aquaculture/Veterinary
Trimethoprim[a]	0.005	64-75-5	diaminopyrimidine antibiotic	Human/Veterinary
Carbamazepine[a]	0.005	298-46-4	anticonvulsant	Human
Ibuprofen[a]	0.050	15687-27-1	antiinflammatory	Human

[a] Preferred method of analysis for this analyte (see table 3 for secondary method of analysis).

of the investigation (February to August 2005) were also analyzed for dissolved organic carbon according to methods described in Wershaw and others (1987).

Quality Assurance and Quality Control

Concentrations of pharmaceutical compounds and OWCs presented in this report have been evaluated with respect to analysis of laboratory and field blanks, surrogate recoveries, spike recoveries, internal standard responses, and continuing calibration criteria. Many of these compounds are commonly found in the environment and can easily contaminate samples and sampling equipment during collection, processing, and

transport. Several of these compounds have also been identified as common laboratory contaminants (Zaugg and Leiker, 2006). Considerable variation exists in the precision of the three analytical methods used during this study. Likewise, there is considerable variation in the capability of quantifying various analytes for a given method. As a result, concentrations of compounds, such as caffeine and carbamazepine, which were analyzed by more than one method can show variation related to analytical method. Interfering substances, such as dissolved organic carbon, can contribute to errors in quantitation, especially at the low concentrations (less than parts per billion) at which many of these analytes were detected. Concentrations of analytes that were detected but were not within the range of calibration have been flagged as estimated concentrations and are considered semiquantitative. Pharmaceutical compounds and OWCs in effluent and water samples were considered to be not detected if the concentration was less than 10 times the concentration in associated laboratory and field blanks. Failure to detect an analyte indicates that the concentration of the analyte was less than the analytical detection limit rather than the absence of the analyte in the sample.

Phase 1 Results

Samples obtained during the first phase of the study were collected during low streamflow conditions in August and September 2003. Analytical results for pharmaceutical compounds and OWCs in samples of treated effluent collected at WWTPs in the Tar and Cape Fear River basins are provided in tables 6–8. Analytical results for pharmaceutical compounds and OWCs in samples of raw water collected at DWTPs are provided in tables 9–11 for sites in the Tar and Cape Fear River basins.

More pharmaceutical compounds and OWCs were detected in wastewater samples than in raw drinking-water samples. Most of the analytes that were detected occurred at concentrations less than the method detection limit and are presented as estimated concentrations. The most commonly detected pharmaceutical compound in wastewater was carbamazepine, which was detected in all 10 samples (table 6). Other commonly detected pharmaceutical compounds include cotinine (seven samples), diphen hydramine (six samples), dehydronifedipine (four samples), sulfamethoxazole (four samples), and trimethoprim (three samples). No regulatory standards have been established for these pharmaceutical compounds.

Treated Effluent Samples from Wastewater-Treatment Facilities

Various OWCs were detected in the treated effluent samples. Four OWCs—the flame retardant tri(2-chloroethyl) phosphate, the fragrances hexahydrohexamethylcyclopenta-benzopyran (HHCB) and benzophenone, and the plasticizer triethyl citrate—were detected in all of the effluent samples (tables 7 and 8). Other OWCs detected in half or more of the effluent samples include tributyl phosphate (nine samples); bromoform, p-cresol, and methyl salicylate (eight samples); caffeine and tri(dichloroisopropyl) phosphate (six samples); and acetyl-hexamethyl-tetrahydronaphthalene (AHTN), metolachlor, and 5-methyl-1H-benzotriazole (five samples). Concentrations of most OWCs in effluent samples were near or less than reporting limits. Only four analytes—HHCB, p-cresol, tri(dichloroisopropyl) phosphate, and tributyl phosphate—exceeded analytical reporting limits. None of these compounds were present at levels that exceeded North Carolina surface-water quality criteria.

Raw Water Samples from Drinking-Water Treatment Facilities

Only four of the 24 pharmaceutical compounds listed in table 3 were detected in raw drinking-water samples. Cotinine, a urinary metabolite of nicotine, was detected in all water samples at concentrations ranging from about 0.0049–0.033 microgram per liter (µg/L; table 9). Caffeine was the second most commonly detected pharmaceutical compound and was detected in 9 of 10 samples. Diphenhydramine (4 of 10 samples) and carbamazepine (3 of 10 samples) also were detected in raw water samples. Drinking-water standards have not been established for these analytes, and concentrations of most of those that were detected were less than the range of calibration.

Several OWCs were detected in raw water samples from DWTPs in the Tar and Cape Fear River basins (tables 10 and 11, respectively). Methyl salicylate and benzophenone (and caffeine, using the secondary analytical method) were the most commonly detected OWCs and were detected in 9 of 10 samples. Metolachlor was detected in 8 samples, and p-cresol and octylphenol diethoxylates (OP2EO) were detected in 6 of 10 raw water samples. The flame retardants tri(2-chloroethyl) phosphate, tributyl phosphate, and tri(dichloroisopropyl) phosphate were detected only in samples from DWTPs in the Cape Fear River basin. None of the OWCs were detected at concentrations that exceeded North Carolina water-quality criteria (table 4).

Table 6. Concentrations of selected pharmaceutical compounds in samples of treated effluent from municipal wastewater-treatment facilities in the Tar and Cape Fear River basins, North Carolina, September 2003.

[μg/L, microgram per liter; <, less than; RL, reporting limit; analytes with known or suspected hormonal activity are shown in **bold** type; the method of analysis for data presented in this table is described in Cahill and others (2004)]

Site identifier (tables 1, 2; figs. 2, 3)	Tar River basin			Cape Fear River basin						
	Tar-WW01	Tar-WW02	Tar-WW03	CF-WW01	CF-WW02	CF-WW03	CF-WW04	CFWW-05	CF-WW06	CFWW-07
Date sample collected	09/11/03	09/05/03	09/05/03	09/12/03	09/09/03	09/12/03	09/10/03	09/10/03	09/09/03	09/10/03
Analyte (μg/L)										
Acetaminophen	0.0074[a]	<RL	<RL	<RL	<RL	<RL	<RL	<RL	0.0092	<RL
Albuterol	<RL	<RL	<RL	<RL	<RL	<RL	<RL	<RL	<RL	<RL
Azithromycin[b]	<RL	<RL	<RL	<RL	<RL	<RL	<RL	<RL	<RL	<RL
Caffeine[c]	<RL	<RL	<RL	1.7	<RL	<RL	<RL	<RL	0.050	<RL
Carbamazepine[b]	0.078	0.027	0.17	0.061	0.15	0.11	0.060	0.053	0.12	0.19
Cimetidine	0.056	<RL	<RL	<RL	0.028	0.17	<RL	<RL	<RL	<RL
Codeine	<RL	0.0081[a]	<RL	0.042	<RL	0.025	<RL	<RL	<RL	<RL
Cotinine[c]	0.041	<RL	<RL	<RL	0.0096	0.022	0.028	0.0080	0.055	0.027
Dehydronifedipine	0.011	<RL	0.0025[a]	<RL	0.0056[a]	0.0089[a]	0.028	<RL	<RL	<RL
Diltiazem	<RL	<RL	<RL	<RL	0.0045[a]	0.028	<RL	<RL	<RL	<RL
1,7-Dimethylxanthine	0.17	<RL	<RL	<RL	<RL	<RL	<RL	<RL	<RL	<RL
Diphenhydramine[b]	0.035	0.022	<RL	0.037	<RL	0.028	0.038	<RL	<RL	0.059
Erythromycin[b]	<RL	<RL	<RL	<RL	<RL	<RL	<RL	<RL	<RL	<RL
Fluoxetine	**<RL**	**<RL**	**<RL**	**<RL**	**<RL**	**<RL**	**<RL**	**<RL**	**<RL**	**<RL**
Furosemide	<RL	<RL	<RL	<RL	<RL	<RL	<RL	<RL	<RL	<RL
Gemfibrozil	<RL	<RL	<RL	<RL	<RL	<RL	<RL	<RL	<RL	<RL
Ibuprofen	<RL	<RL	<RL	<RL	<RL	<RL	<RL	<RL	<RL	<RL
Metformin	<RL	<RL	<RL	<RL	<RL	<RL	<RL	<RL	<RL	<RL
Miconazole[b]	<RL	<RL	<RL	<RL	<RL	<RL	<RL	<RL	<RL	<RL
Ranitidine	<RL	<RL	<RL	<RL	0.016	<RL	<RL	<RL	<RL	<RL
Sulfamethoxazole	<RL	<RL	0.15	<RL	0.23	0.18	0.099	<RL	<RL	<RL
Thiabendazole[b]	<RL	<RL	<RL	<RL	<RL	<RL	<RL	<RL	<RL	<RL
Trimethoprim	0.0037[a]	<RL	<RL	<RL	0.0097	0.071	<RL	<RL	<RL	<RL
Warfarin	<RL	<RL	<RL	<RL	<RL	<RL	<RL	<RL	<RL	<RL

[a] Estimated concentration (analyte detected at a concentration outside the range of calibration).

[b] Method detection limit not established at time of analysis.

[c] Preferred method of analysis for this analyte (see tables 7 and 8 for secondary method of analysis).

Table 7. Concentrations of selected organic wastewater compounds in treated effluent from municipal wastewater-treatment facilities in the Tar River basin, North Carolina, September 2003

[µg/L, microgram per liter; <, less than; PAH, polycyclic aromatic hydrocarbon; analytes with known or suspected hormonal activity are shown in **bold** type; the method of analysis for data presented in this table corresponds to that described in Zaugg and others (2002)]

Site identifier (table 1; fig. 2)	Tar-WW01	Tar-WW02	Tar-WW03
Date sample collected	**9/11/2003**	**9/5/2003**	**9/5/2003**
Analyte (µg/L)			
Detergent components and degradates			
4-Cumylphenol	<1.0	<1.0	<1.0
***p*-Nonylphenol (total)**	<5.0	<5.0	<5.0
Nonylphenol diethoxylates (NP2EO)	<5.0	<5.0	<5.0
4-*n*-Octylphenol	<1.0	<1.0	<1.0
4-*t*-Octylphenol	<1.0	<1.0	<1.0
4-*t*-Octylphenol monoethoxylates (OP1EO)	<1.0	<1.0	<1.0
4-*t*-Octylphenol diethoxylates (OP2EO)	<1.0	<1.0	<1.0
Flame retardants			
Tributyl phosphate	0.20[a]	0.33[a]	0.07[a]
Tri(2-chloroethyl) phosphate	0.2[a]	0.2[a]	0.2[a]
Tri(dichloroisopropyl) phosphate	0.6	<0.5	<0.5
Triphenyl phosphate	<0.5	<0.5	<0.5
Fragrances			
Acetophenone	0.22[a]	<0.5	0.12[a]
Benzophenone	**0.18[a]**	**0.09[a]**	**0.05[a]**
1,3,4,6,7,8-Hexahydro-4,6,6,7,8,8-hexamethyl-cyclopenta-γ-2-benzopyran (HHCB)	**0.79**	**0.08[a]**	**0.14[a]**
Indole	<0.5	0.02[a]	<0.5
3-Methyl-1H-indole (skatole)	0.02[a]	<1.0	<1.0
Isoborneol	<0.5	<0.5	<0.5
Menthol	<0.5	<0.5	<0.5
Methyl salicylate	0.04[a]	0.02[a]	0.02[a]
7-Acetyl-1,1,3,4,4,6-hexamethyl-1,2,3,4-tetrahydronaphthalene (AHTN)	**0.04[a]**	**<0.5**	**<0.5**
PAHs, fossil fuel components, combustion byproducts			
Anthracene	<0.5	<0.5	<0.5
Anthraquinone	0.08[a]	<0.5	<0.5
p-Cresol	<1.0	0.3[a]	0.08[a]
Fluoranthene	<0.5	<0.5	<0.5
Naphthalene	<0.5	<0.5	<0.5
1-Methylnaphthalene	<0.5	<0.5	<0.5
2-Methylnaphthalene	<0.5	<0.5	<0.5
2,6-Dimethylnaphthalene	<0.5	<0.5	<0.5
Phenanthrene	<0.5	<0.5	<0.5
Pyrene	**<0.5**	**<0.5**	**<0.5**
Benzo[*a*]pyrene	**<0.5**	**<0.5**	**<0.5**
Pesticides			
Bromacil	**<0.5**	**<0.5**	**<0.5**
Carbaryl	**<1.0**	**<1.0**	**0.2[a]**
Carbazole	<0.5	<0.5	<0.5
Chlorpyrifos	**<0.5**	**<0.5**	**<0.5**
Diazinon	**<0.5**	**<0.5**	**<0.5**
d-**Dichlorvos**	**<1.0**	**<1.0**	**<1.0**
d-Limonene	<0.5	<0.5	<0.5
Metalaxyl	<0.5	<0.5	<0.5
Metolachlor	<0.5	<0.5	0.02[a]
Pentachlorophenol	**0.6[a]**	**<2.0**	**<2.0**
Prometon	<0.5	<0.5	<0.5
Pharmaceutical compounds or metabolites			
Caffeine[b]	0.07[a]	0.04[a]	<0.5
Cotinine[b]	0.4[a]	<1.0	<1.0
Isoquinoline	<0.5	<0.5	<0.5

Table 7. Concentrations of selected organic wastewater compounds in treated effluent from municipal wastewater-treatment facilities in the Tar River basin, North Carolina, September 2003.—Continued

[μg/L, microgram per liter; <, less than; PAH, polycyclic aromatic hydrocarbon; analytes with known or suspected hormonal activity are shown in **bold** type; the method of analysis for data presented in this table corresponds to that described in Zaugg and others (2002)]

Site identifier (table 1; fig. 2)	Tar-WW01	Tar-WW02	Tar-WW03
Date sample collected	9/11/2003	9/5/2003	9/5/2003
Analyte (μg/L)			
Plasticizers			
Bisphenol A	**<1.0**	**<1.0**	**<1.0**
Camphor	<0.5	<0.5	<0.5
Triethyl citrate (ethyl citrate)	0.14[a]	0.14[a]	0.1[a]
Tri(2-butoxyethyl) phosphate	<0.5	0.3[a]	<0.5
Solvents			
Isophorone	0.02[a]	<0.5	<0.5
Isopropylbenzene (cumene)	<0.5	<0.5	<0.5
Tetrachloroethylene (PCE)	<0.5	<0.5	<0.5
Biogenic sterols			
Cholesterol	0.8[a]	<2.0	<2.0
3-β-Coprostanol	0.2[a]	<2.0	<2.0
β-Sitosterol	**<2.0**	**<2.0**	**<2.0**
β-Stigmastanol	<2.0	<2.0	<2.0
Miscellaneous compounds			
3-t-Butyl-4-hydroxyanisole (BHA)	**<5.0**	**<5.0**	**<5.0**
1,4-Dichlorobenzene	**<0.5**	**<0.5**	**<0.5**
5-Methyl-1H-benzotriazole	<2.0	1.4[a]	0.8[a]
Bromoform	<0.5	0.14[a]	0.60[a]
Triclosan	**<1.0**	**<1.0**	**<1.0**

[a] Estimated concentration (analyte detected at a concentration outside the range of calibration).

[b] Secondary method of analysis for this analyte (see table 6 for preferred method of analysis).

Table 8. Concentrations of selected organic wastewater compounds in treated effluent from municipal wastewater-treatment facilities in the Cape Fear River basin, North Carolina, September 2003

[µg/L, microgram per liter; <, less than; analytes with known or suspected hormonal activity are shown in **bold** type; the method of analysis for data presented in this table corresponds to that described in Zaugg and others (2002)]

Site identifier (table 1; fig. 3)	CF-WW01	CF-WW02	CF-WW03	CF-WW04	CF-WW05	CF-WW06	CF-WW07
Date sample collected	09/13/03	09/12/03	09/09/03	09/10/03	09/10/03	09/09/03	09/09/03
Analyte (µg/L)							
Detergent components and degradates							
4-Cumylphenol	<1.0	<1.0	<1.0	<1.0	<1.0	<1.0	<1.0
p-Nonylphenol (total)	<5.0	1.4[a]	<5.0	<5.0	<5.0	<5.0	<5.0
Nonylphenol diethoxylates (NP2EO)	<5.0	2.8[a]	<5.0	<5.0	<5.0	<5.0	<5.0
4-n-Octylphenol	<1.0	<1.0	<1.0	<1.0	<1.0	<1.0	<1.0
4-t-Octylphenol	<1.0	0.09[a]	<1.0	<1.0	<1.0	<1.0	<1.0
4-t-Octylphenol monoethoxylates (OP1EO)	<1.0	<1.0	<1.0	<1.0	<1.0	<1.0	<1.0
4-t-Octylphenol diethoxylates (OP2EO)	<1.0	<1.0	<1.0	<1.0	0.1[a]	<1.0	<1.0
Flame retardants							
Tri(2-chloroethyl) phosphate	0.3[a]	0.2[a]	0.4[a]	0.3[a]	0.2[a]	0.3[a]	0.3[a]
Tri(dichloroisopropyl) phosphate	0.07[a]	0.12[a]	0.32[a]	<0.5	0.06[a]	0.17[a]	<0.5
Tributyl phosphate	0.51	0.18[a]	0.08[a]	0.19[a]	<0.5	0.09[a]	0.20[a]
Triphenyl phosphate	<0.5	<0.5	<0.5	<0.5	<0.5	<0.5	<0.5
Fragrances							
Acetophenone	<0.5	<0.5	<0.5	<0.5	<0.5	<0.5	<0.5
Benzophenone	0.11[a]	0.30[a]	0.09[a]	0.09[a]	0.06[a]	0.10[a]	0.15[a]
1,3,4,6,7,8-Hexahydro-4,6,6,7,8,8-hexamethylcyclopenta-γ-2-benzopyran (HHCB)	0.20[a]	0.43[a]	0.38[a]	0.10[a]	0.15[a]	0.14[a]	0.09[a]
Indole	<0.5	<0.5	<0.5	<0.5	<0.5	<0.5	<0.5
3-Methyl-1H-indole (skatole)	<1.0	<1.0	<1.0	<1.0	<1.0	<1.0	<1.0
Isoborneol	<0.5	<0.5	<0.5	<0.5	<0.5	<0.5	<0.5
Menthol	<0.5	<0.5	<0.5	<0.5	<0.5	0.02[a]	<0.5
Methyl salicylate	<0.5	0.03[a]	0.02[a]	0.02[a]	0.02[a]	0.02[a]	<0.5
7-Acetyl-1,1,3,4,4,6-hexamethyl-1,2,3,4-tetrahydronaphthalene (AHTN)	<0.5	0.13[a]	0.06[a]	<0.5	0.02[a]	0.02[a]	<0.5
PAHs, fossil fuel components, combustion byproducts							
Anthracene	<0.5	<0.5	<0.5	<0.5	<0.5	<0.5	<0.5
Anthraquinone	<0.5	0.10[a]	<0.5	<0.5	<0.5	<0.5	<0.5
p-Cresol	<1.0	1.2	0.02[a]	0.06[a]	0.05[a]	0.03[a]	0.09[a]
Fluoranthene	<0.5	<0.5	<0.5	<0.5	<0.5	<0.5	<0.5
Naphthalene	<0.5	<0.5	<0.5	<0.5	<0.5	<0.5	<0.5
1-Methylnaphthalene	<0.5	<0.5	<0.5	<0.5	<0.5	<0.5	<0.5
2-Methylnaphthalene	<0.5	<0.5	<0.5	<0.5	<0.5	<0.5	<0.5
2,6-Dimethylnaphthalene	<0.5	<0.5	<0.5	<0.5	<0.5	<0.5	<0.5
Phenanthrene	<0.5	<0.5	<0.5	<0.5	<0.5	<0.5	<0.5
Pyrene	<0.5	<0.5	<0.5	<0.5	<0.5	<0.5	<0.5
Benzo[a]pyrene	<0.5	<0.5	<0.5	<0.5	<0.5	<0.5	<0.5

Table 8. Concentrations of selected organic wastewater compounds in treated effluent from municipal wastewater-treatment facilities in the Cape Fear River basin, North Carolina, September 2003.—Continued

[μg/L, microgram per liter; <, less than; analytes with known or suspected hormonal activity are shown in **bold** type; the method of analysis for data presented in this table corresponds to that described in Zaugg and others (2002)]

Site identifier (table 1; fig. 3)	CF-WW01	CF-WW02	CF-WW03	CF-WW04	CF-WW05	CF-WW06	CF-WW07
Date sample collected	09/13/03	09/12/03	09/09/03	09/10/03	09/10/03	09/09/03	09/09/03
Analyte (μg/L)							
Pesticides							
Bromacil	<0.5	<0.5	<0.5	<0.5	<0.5	<0.5	<0.5
Carbaryl	<1.0	<1.0	<1.0	<1.0	<1.0	<1.0	<1.0
Carbazole	<0.5	<0.5	<0.5	<0.5	<0.5	<0.5	<0.5
Chlorpyrifos	<0.5	<0.5	<0.5	<0.5	<0.5	<0.5	<0.5
Diazinon	<0.5	<0.5	0.08[a]	<0.5	<0.5	<0.5	<0.5
d-**Dichlorvos**	<1.0	<1.0	<1.0	<1.0	<1.0	<1.0	<1.0
d-Limonene	<0.5	<0.5	<0.5	<0.5	<0.5	<0.5	<0.5
Metalaxyl	<0.5	<0.5	<0.5	<0.5	<0.5	<0.5	<0.5
Metolachlor	<0.5	<0.5	0.03[a]	<0.5	0.03[a]	0.11[a]	0.09[a]
Pentachlorophenol	<2.0	<2.0	0.2[a]	0.6[a]	0.4[a]	<2.0	<2.0
Prometon	<0.5	<0.5	<0.5	<0.5	<0.5	<0.5	<0.5
Pharmaceutical compounds or metabolites							
Caffeine[b]	0.07[a]	0.05[a]	0.03[a]	<0.5	<0.5	0.10[a]	<0.5
Cotinine[b]	<1.0	<1.0	<1.0	0.4[a]	<1.0	0.1[a]	<1.0
Isoquinoline	<0.5	0.24[a]	<0.5	<0.5	<0.5	<0.5	<0.5
Plasticizers							
Bisphenol A	<1.0	<1.0	<1.0	<1.0	<1.0	<1.0	<1.0
Camphor	<0.5	<0.5	<0.5	<0.5	<0.5	<0.5	<0.5
Triethyl citrate (ethyl citrate)	0.24[a]	0.15[a]	0.03[a]	0.16[a]	0.05[a]	0.08[a]	0.14[a]
Tri(2-butoxyethyl) phosphate	0.34[a]	<0.5	<0.5	<0.5	0.33[a]	<0.5	<0.5
Solvents							
Isophorone	<0.5	<0.5	<0.5	<0.5	<0.5	<0.5	<0.5
Isopropylbenzene (cumene)	<0.5	<0.5	<0.5	<0.5	<0.5	<0.5	<0.5
Tetrachloroethylene (PCE)	<0.5	<0.5	<0.5	<0.5	<0.5	<0.5	<0.5
Biogenic sterols							
Cholesterol	<2.0	0.8[a]	<2.0	0.9[a]	<2.0	<2.0	<2.0
3-β-Coprostanol	<2.0	<2.0	<2.0	0.2[a]	<2.0	<2.0	<2.0
β-Sitosterol	<2.0	<2.0	<2.0	<2.0	<2.0	<2.0	<2.0
β-Stigmastanol	<2.0	<2.0	<2.0	<2.0	<2.0	<2.0	<2.0
Miscellaneous compounds							
3-*t*-Butyl-4-hydroxyanisole (BHA)	<5.0	<5.0	<5.0	<5.0	<5.0	<5.0	<5.0
1,4-Dichlorobenzene	<0.5	<0.5	0.04[a]	<0.5	<0.5	<0.5	<0.5
5-Methyl-1H-benzotriazole	<2.0	<2.0	0.9[a]	<2.0	1.0[a]	1.0[a]	<2.0
Bromoform	<0.5	0.07[a]	0.02[a]	0.42[a]	0.06[a]	0.12[a]	0.15[a]
Triclosan	<1.0	<1.0	0.1[a]	<1.0	<1.0	<1.0	<1.0

[a] Estimated concentration (analyte detected at a concentration outside the range of calibration).

[b] Secondary method of analysis for this analyte (see table 6 for preferred method of analysis).

Table 9. Concentrations of selected pharmaceutical compounds in raw water from municipal drinking-water treatment facilities in the Tar and Cape Fear River basins, North Carolina, August–September 2003.

[µg/L, microgram per liter; <, less than; RL, reporting limit; analytes with known or suspected hormonal activity are shown in **bold** type; the method of analysis for data presented in this table corresponds to that described in Cahill and others (2004)]

Site identifier (table 2; figs. 2, 3)	Tar River basin			Cape Fear River basin						
	Tar-DW01	Tar-DW02	Tar-DW03	CF-DW01	CF-DW02	CF-DW03	CF-DW04	CF-DW05	CF-DW06	CF-DW07
Date sample collected	09/05/03	09/05/03	09/05/03	09/09/03	09/09/03	09/10/03	09/09/03	09/10/03	09/10/03	08/28/03
Analyte (µg/L)										
Acetaminophen	<RL	<RL	<RL	<RL	<RL	<RL	<RL	<RL	<RL	<RL
Albuterol	<RL	<RL	<RL	<RL	<RL	<RL	<RL	<RL	<RL	<RL
Azithromycin[a]	<RL	<RL	<RL	<RL	<RL	<RL	<RL	<RL	<RL	<RL
Caffeine[b]	<RL	0.0038[c]	0.0051[c]	0.031	0.0088	0.014	0.0077	0.020	0.035	0.0068[c]
Carbamazepine[a]	<RL	<RL	<RL	<RL	0.0060	0.0038[c]	<RL	0.004[c]	<RL	<RL
Cimetidine	<RL	<RL	<RL	<RL	<RL	<RL	<RL	<RL	<RL	<RL
Codeine	<RL	<RL	<RL	<RL	<RL	<RL	<RL	<RL	<RL	<RL
Cotinine[b]	0.016	0.014	0.033	0.013	0.011	0.016	0.013	0.017	0.015	0.0049[c]
Dehydronifedipine	<RL	<RL	<RL	<RL	<RL	<RL	<RL	<RL	<RL	<RL
Diltiazem	<RL	<RL	<RL	<RL	<RL	<RL	<RL	<RL	<RL	<RL
1,7-Dimethylxanthine	<RL	<RL	<RL	<RL	<RL	<RL	<RL	<RL	<RL	<RL
Diphenhydramine[a]	<RL	<RL	<RL	<RL	0.011	0.0032[c]	0.0011[c]	<RL	0.003	<RL
Erythromycin[a]	<RL	<RL	<RL	<RL	<RL	<RL	<RL	<RL	<RL	<RL
Fluoxetine	**<RL**	**<RL**	**<RL**	**<RL**	**<RL**	**<RL**	**<RL**	**<RL**	**<RL**	**<RL**
Furosemide	<RL	<RL	<RL	<RL	<RL	<RL	<RL	<RL	<RL	<RL
Gemfibrozil	<RL	<RL	<RL	<RL	<RL	<RL	<RL	<RL	<RL	<RL
Ibuprofen	<RL	<RL	<RL	<RL	<RL	<RL	<RL	<RL	<RL	<RL
Metformin	<RL	<RL	<RL	<RL	<RL	<RL	<RL	<RL	<RL	<RL
Miconazole[a]	<RL	<RL	<RL	<RL	<RL	<RL	<RL	<RL	<RL	<RL
Ranitidine	<RL	<RL	<RL	<RL	<RL	<RL	<RL	<RL	<RL	<RL
Sulfamethoxazole	<RL	<RL	<RL	<RL	<RL	<RL	<RL	<RL	<RL	<RL
Thiabendazole[a]	<RL	<RL	<RL	<RL	<RL	<RL	<RL	<RL	<RL	<RL
Trimethoprim	<RL	<RL	<RL	<RL	<RL	<RL	<RL	<RL	<RL	<RL
Warfarin	<RL	<RL	<RL	<RL	<RL	<RL	<RL	<RL	<RL	<RL

[a] Method detection limit not established at time of analysis.

[b] Preferred method of analysis for this analyte (see tables 10 and 11 for secondary method of analysis).

[c] Estimated concentration (analyte detected at a concentration outside the range of calibration).

Table 10. Concentrations of selected organic wastewater compounds in raw water samples from municipal drinking-water treatment facilities in the Tar River basin, North Carolina, September 2003

[µg/L, microgram per liter; <, less than; PAH, polycyclic aromatic hydrocarbon; analytes with known or suspected hormonal activity are shown in **bold** type; the method of analysis for data presented in this table corresponds to that described in Zaugg and others (2002)]

Site identifier (table 2; fig. 2)	Tar-DW01	Tar-DW02	Tar-DW03
Date sample collected	09/05/03	09/05/03	09/05/03
Analyte (µg/L)			
Detergent components and degradates			
4-Cumylphenol	<1.0	<1.0	<1.0
***p*-Nonylphenol (total)**	<5.0	<5.0	<5.0
Nonylphenol diethoxylates (NP2EO)	<5.0	<5.0	<5.0
4-*n*-Octylphenol	<1.0	<1.0	<1.0
4-*t*-Octylphenol	<1.0	<1.0	<1.0
4-*t*-Octylphenol monoethoxylates (OP1EO)	<1.0	<1.0	<1.0
4-*t*-Octylphenol diethoxylates (OP2EO)	0.1[a]	0.1[a]	0.1[a]
Flame retardants			
Tributyl phosphate	<0.5	<0.5	<0.5
Tri(2-chloroethyl) phosphate	<0.5	<0.5	<0.5
Tri(dichloroisopropyl) phosphate	<0.5	<0.5	<0.5
Triphenyl phosphate	<0.5	<0.5	<0.5
Fragrances			
Acetophenone	<0.5	<0.5	<0.5
Benzophenone	0.02[a]	0.02[a]	<0.5
1,3,4,6,7,8-Hexahydro-4,6,6,7,8,8-hexamethylcyclopenta-γ-2-benzopyran (HHCB)	<0.5	<0.5	<0.5
Indole	0.03[a]	<0.5	<0.5
3-Methyl-1H-indole (skatole)	<1.0	<1.0	<1.0
Isoborneol	<0.5	<0.5	<0.5
Menthol	<0.5	<0.5	<0.5
Methyl salicylate	0.03[a]	0.03[a]	0.03[a]
7-Acetyl-1,1,3,4,4,6-hexamethyl-1,2,3,4-tetrahydronaphthalene (AHTN)	<0.5	<0.5	<0.5
PAHs, fossil fuel components, combustion byproducts			
Anthracene	<0.5	<0.5	<0.5
Anthraquinone	<0.5	<0.5	<0.5
p-Cresol	0.08[a]	0.02[a]	<1.0
Fluoranthene	<0.5	<0.5	<0.5
Naphthalene	<0.5	<0.5	<0.5
1-Methylnaphthalene	<0.5	<0.5	<0.5
2-Methylnaphthalene	<0.5	<0.5	<0.5
2,6-Dimethylnaphthalene	<0.5	<0.5	<0.5
Phenanthrene	<0.5	<0.5	<0.5
Pyrene	<0.5	<0.5	<0.5
Benzo[*a*]pyrene	<0.5	<0.5	<0.5
Pesticides			
Bromacil	<0.5	<0.5	<0.5
Carbaryl	<1.0	<1.0	0.08[a]
Carbazole	<0.5	<0.5	<0.5
Chlorpyrifos	<0.5	<0.5	<0.5
Diazinon	<0.5	<0.5	<0.5
***d*-Dichlorvos**	<1.0	<1.0	<1.0
d-Limonene	<0.5	<0.5	<0.5
Metalaxyl	<0.5	<0.5	<0.5
Metolachlor	0.02[a]	<0.5	0.07[a]
Pentachlorophenol	<2.0	<2.0	0.3[a]
Prometon	<0.5	<0.5	<0.5

Table 10. Concentrations of selected organic wastewater compounds in raw water samples from municipal drinking-water treatment facilities in the Tar River basin, North Carolina, September 2003.—Continued

[µg/L, microgram per liter; <, less than; PAH, polycyclic aromatic hydrocarbon; analytes with known or suspected hormonal activity are shown in **bold** type; the method of analysis for data presented in this table corresponds to that described in Zaugg and others (2002)]

Site identifier (table 2; fig. 2)	Tar-DW01	Tar-DW02	Tar-DW03
Date sample collected	09/05/03	09/05/03	09/05/03
Analyte (µg/L)			
Pharmaceuticals			
Caffeine[b]	0.02[a]	0.02[a]	0.03[a]
Cotinine[b]	<1.0	<1.0	<1.0
Isoquinoline	<0.5	<0.5	<0.5
Plasticizers			
Bisphenol A	**<1.0**	**<1.0**	**<1.0**
Camphor	<0.5	<0.5	0.02[a]
Triethyl citrate (ethyl citrate)	<0.5	<0.5	<0.5
Tri(2-butoxyethyl) phosphate	<0.5	<0.5	<0.5
Solvents			
Isophorone	<0.5	<0.5	<0.5
Isopropylbenzene (cumene)	<0.5	<0.5	<0.5
Tetrachloroethylene (PCE)	<0.5	<0.5	<0.5
Biogenic sterols			
Cholesterol	<2.0	<2.0	<2.0
3-β-Coprostanol	<2.0	<2.0	<2.0
β-Sitosterol	**<2.0**	**<2.0**	**<2.0**
β-Stigmastanol	<2.0	<2.0	<2.0
Miscellaneous compounds			
3-*t*-Butyl-4-hydroxyanisole (BHA)	**<5.0**	**<5.0**	**<5.0**
1,4-Dichlorobenzene	**<0.5**	**<0.5**	**<0.5**
5-Methyl-1H-benzotriazole	<2.0	<2.0	<2.0
Bromoform	<0.5	<0.5	<0.5
Triclosan	**<1.0**	**<1.0**	**<1.0**

[a] Estimated concentration (analyte detected at a concentration outside the range of calibration).

[b] Secondary method of analysis for this analyte (see table 9 for the preferred method of analysis).

Table 11. Concentrations of selected organic wastewater compounds in raw water samples from municipal drinking-water treatment facilities in the Cape Fear River basin, North Carolina, August–September 2003.

[µg/L, microgram per liter; <, less than; PAH, polycyclic aromatic hydrocarbon; analytes with known or suspected hormonal activity are shown in **bold** type; the method of analysis for data presented in this table corresponds to that described in Zaugg and others (2002)]

Site identifier (table 2; fig. 3)	CF-DW01	CF-DW02	CF-DW03	CF-DW04	CF-DW05	CF-DW06	CF-DW07
Date sample collected	09/09/03	09/09/03	09/10/03	09/09/03	09/10/03	09/10/03	08/28/03
Analyte (µg/L)							
Detergent components and degradates							
4-Cumylphenol	<1.0	<1.0	<1.0	<1.0	<1.0	<1.0	<1.0
p-Nonylphenol (total)	<5.0	<5.0	<5.0	<5.0	<5.0	<5.0	<5.0
Nonylphenol diethoxylates (NP2EO)	<5.0	<5.0	<5.0	<5.0	<5.0	<5.0	<5.0
4-n-Octylphenol	<1.0	<1.0	<1.0	<1.0	<1.0	<1.0	<1.0
4-t-Octylphenol	<1.0	<1.0	<1.0	<1.0	<1.0	<1.0	<1.0
4-t-Octylphenol monoethoxylates (OP1EO)	0.6[a]	0.6[a]	<1.0	<1.0	<1.0	0.5[a]	<1.0
4-t-Octylphenol diethoxylates (OP2EO)	<1.0	0.1[a]	<1.0	<1.0	0.1[a]	0.08[a]	<1.0
Flame retardants							
Tributyl phosphate	0.03[a]	0.02[a]	0.17[a]	0.02[a]	<0.5	0.19[a]	0.06[a]
Tri(2-chloroethyl) phosphate	0.8	0.4[a]	0.3[a]	0.2a	0.2[a]	0.3[a]	0.2[a]
Tri(dichloroisopropyl) phosphate	<0.5	0.18[a]	<0.5	0.10[a]	0.06[a]	0.05[a]	<0.5
Triphenyl phosphate	<0.5	<0.5	<0.5	<0.5	<0.5	<0.5	<0.5
Fragrances							
Acetophenone	<0.5	<0.5	<0.5	<0.5	<0.5	0.10[a]	0.12[a]
Benzophenone	0.02[a]	0.02[a]	0.08[a]	0.03[a]	0.06[a]	0.08[a]	0.04[a]
1,3,4,6,7,8-Hexahydro-4,6,6,7,8,8-hexamethylcyclopenta-γ-2-benzopyran (HHCB)	0.02[a]	<0.5	<0.5	<0.5	0.15[a]	<0.5	<0.5
Indole	<0.5	<0.5	<0.5	<0.5	<0.5	<0.5	<0.5
3-Methyl-1H-indole (skatole)	<1.0	<1.0	<1.0	<1.0	<1.0	<1.0	<1.0
Isoborneol	<0.5	<0.5	<0.5	<0.5	<0.5	<0.5	<0.5
Menthol	<0.5	<0.5	<0.5	<0.5	<0.5	<0.5	<0.5
Methyl salicylate	0.03[a]	0.03[a]	<0.5	0.04[a]	0.02[a]	0.04[a]	0.09[a]
7-Acetyl-1,1,3,4,4,6-hexamethyl-1,2,3,4-tetrahydronaphthalene (AHTN)	<0.5	<0.5	<0.5	<0.5	0.016[a]	<0.5	<0.5
PAHs, fossil fuel components, combustion byproducts							
Anthracene	<0.5	<0.5	<0.5	<0.5	<0.5	<0.5	<0.5
Anthraquinone	<0.5	<0.5	<0.5	<0.5	<0.5	<0.5	<0.5
p-Cresol	0.02[a]	0.03[a]	<1.0	<1.0	0.05[a]	<1.0	0.03[a]
Fluoranthene	<0.5	<0.5	<0.5	<0.5	<0.5	<0.5	<0.5
Naphthalene	<0.5	<0.5	<0.5	<0.5	<0.5	<0.5	<0.5
1-Methylnaphthalene	<0.5	<0.5	<0.5	<0.5	<0.5	<0.5	<0.5
2-Methylnaphthalene	<0.5	<0.5	<0.5	<0.5	<0.5	<0.5	<0.5
2,6-Dimethylnaphthalene	<0.5	<0.5	<0.5	<0.5	<0.5	<0.5	<0.5
Phenanthrene	<0.5	<0.5	<0.5	<0.5	<0.5	<0.5	<0.5
Pyrene	<0.5	<0.5	<0.5	<0.5	<0.5	<0.5	<0.5
Benzo[a]pyrene	<0.5	<0.5	<0.5	<0.5	<0.5	<0.5	<0.5
Pesticides							
Bromacil	<0.5	<0.5	<0.5	<0.5	<0.5	<0.5	<0.5
Carbaryl	<1.0	<1.0	<1.0	<1.0	<1.0	<1.0	<1.0
Carbazole	<0.5	<0.5	<0.5	<0.5	<0.5	<0.5	<0.5
Chlorpyrifos	<0.5	<0.5	<0.5	<0.5	<0.5	<0.5	<0.5
Diazinon	<0.5	<0.5	<0.5	<0.5	<0.5	<0.5	<0.5
d-Dichlorvos	<1.0	<1.0	<1.0	<1.0	<1.0	<1.0	<1.0

Table 11. Concentrations of selected organic wastewater compounds in raw water samples from municipal drinking-water treatment facilities in the Cape Fear River basin, North Carolina, August–September 2003.—Continued

[μg/L, microgram per liter; <, less than; PAH, polycyclic aromatic hydrocarbon; analytes with known or suspected hormonal activity are shown in **bold** type; the method of analysis for data presented in this table corresponds to that described in Zaugg and others (2002)]

Site identifier (table 2; fig. 3)	CF-DW01	CF-DW02	CF-DW03	CF-DW04	CF-DW05	CF-DW06	CF-DW07
Date sample collected	09/09/03	09/09/03	09/10/03	09/09/03	09/10/03	09/10/03	08/28/03
Analyte (μg/L)							
d-Limonene	<0.5	<0.5	<0.5	<0.5	<0.5	<0.5	<0.5
Metalaxyl	<0.5	<0.5	<0.5	<0.5	<0.5	<0.5	<0.5
Metolachlor	0.12[a]	<0.5	0.06[a]	0.04[a]	0.03[a]	0.08[a]	0.02[a]
Pentachlorophenol	**<2.0**	**<2.0**	**<2.0**	**<2.0**	**0.4[a]**	**<2.0**	**<2.0**
Prometon	<0.5	0.04[a]	<0.5	0.03[a]	<0.5	<0.5	<0.5
Pharmaceutical compounds and metabolites							
Caffeine[b]	0.02[a]	0.05[a]	0.04[a]	0.04[a]	<0.5	0.07[a]	0.03[a]
Cotinine[b]	<1.0	<1.0	<1.0	<1.0	<1.0	<1.0	<1.0
Isoquinoline	<0.5	<0.5	<0.5	<0.5	<0.5	<0.5	<0.5
Plasticizers							
Bisphenol A	**<1.0**	**<1.0**	**<1.0**	**<1.0**	**<1.0**	**0.1[a]**	**<1.0**
Camphor	<0.5	<0.5	<0.5	<0.5	<0.5	<0.5	<0.5
Triethyl citrate (ethyl citrate)	<0.5	<0.5	<0.5	<0.5	0.05[a]	0.13[a]	<0.5
Tri(2-butoxyethyl) phosphate	<0.5	<0.5	<0.5	<0.5	0.33[a]	<0.5	<0.5
Solvents							
Isophorone	<0.5	<0.5	<0.5	<0.5	<0.5	<0.5	<0.5
Isopropylbenzene (cumene)	<0.5	<0.5	<0.5	<0.5	<0.5	<0.5	<0.5
Tetrachloroethylene (PCE)	<0.5	<0.5	<0.5	<0.5	<0.5	<0.5	<0.5
Biogenic sterols							
Cholesterol	<2.0	<2.0	<2.0	<2.0	<2.0	<2.0	<2.0
3-β-Coprostanol	<2.0	<2.0	<2.0	<2.0	<2.0	<2.0	<2.0
β-Sitosterol	**<2.0**	**<2.0**	**<2.0**	**<2.0**	**<2.0**	**<2.0**	**<2.0**
β-Stigmastanol	<2.0	<2.0	<2.0	<2.0	<2.0	<2.0	<2.0
Miscellaneous compounds							
3-*t*-Butyl-4-hydroxyanisole (BHA)	**<5.0**	**<5.0**	**<5.0**	**<5.0**	**<5.0**	**<5.0**	**<5.0**
1,4-Dichlorobenzene	**<0.5**	**<0.5**	**<0.5**	**<0.5**	**<0.5**	**<0.5**	**<0.5**
5-Methyl-1H-benzotriazole	<2.0	<2.0	<2.0	<2.0	1.0[a]	<2.0	<2.0
Bromoform	<0.5	<0.5	<0.5	<0.5	0.06[a]	<0.5	<0.5
Triclosan	**<1.0**	**<1.0**	**<1.0**	**<1.0**	**<1.0**	**<1.0**	**<1.0**

[a] Estimated concentration (analyte detected at a concentration outside the range of calibration).

[b] Secondary method of analysis for this analyte (see table 9 for preferred method of analysis).

Phase 2 Results

Samples obtained during the second phase of the study were collected from February to August 2005. Analytical results for pharmaceutical compounds, OWCs, and antibiotics in samples of treated effluent collected before and after disinfection at two WWTPs in the Tar River basin and two WWTPs in the Cape Fear River basin are provided in tables 12–14. Analytical results for pharmaceutical compounds, OWCs, and antibiotics in samples of water collected at various stages of treatment from two DWTPs in the Tar River basin and three DWTPs in the Cape Fear River basin are provided in tables 15–20. Because of the length of time required for the various drinking-water treatment processes, the initial composition of water samples collected at various stages of treatment may differ from that of the concurrently collected raw water samples. Thus, observed differences in composition may be due to differences in initial composition as well as to effects of treatment. Analytical results for samples collected during the second phase of the study showed that concentrations of pharmaceutical compounds and OWCs were higher in treated wastewater effluent than in the raw drinking-water samples. Most detections were at concentrations near or less than analytical reporting limits.

Effluent Samples Before and After Disinfection at Wastewater-Treatment Facilities

Treated effluent samples collected before and after disinfection contained pharmaceutical compounds, OWCs, and antibiotics (tables 12–14). The pharmaceutical compounds carbamazepine, diltiazem, and diphenhydramine were detected in all samples of wastewater effluent (table 12). Cimetidine, dehydronifedipine, and trimethoprim were also commonly detected in effluent samples (table 12).

Table 12. Concentrations of selected pharmaceutical compounds and metabolites in effluent from municipal wastewater-treatment facilities, before and after disinfection, in the Tar and Cape Fear River basins, North Carolina, May–July 2005.

[UV, ultraviolet; µg/L, microgram per liter; <, less than; MDL, method detection limit; analytes with known or suspected hormonal activity are shown in **bold** type; the method of analysis for data presented in this table corresponds to that described in Cahill and others (2004)]

Site identifier (table 1; figs. 2, 3)	Tar-WW01		Tar-WW03		CF-WW03		CF-WW07	
Disinfection status	before UV irradiation[a]	after UV irradiation[a]	before chlorination	after chlorination	before UV irradiation	after UV irradiation	before chlorination	after chlorination
Date sample collected	05/06/05		07/22/05		06/24/05		07/14/05	
Analyte (µg/L)								
Acetaminophen	<MDL	<MDL	<MDL	<MDL	<MDL	<MDL	<MDL	<MDL
Albuterol	<MDL	<MDL	<MDL	<MDL	<MDL	<MDL	<MDL	<MDL
Azithromycin[b]	<MDL	<MDL	<MDL	<MDL	<MDL	<MDL	<MDL	<MDL
Caffeine[c]	<MDL	<MDL	<MDL	<MDL	<MDL	<MDL	<MDL	<MDL
Carbamazepine[b]	0.132	0.132	0.238	0.266[d]	0.370	0.345	0.219[d]	0.215
Cimetidine	0.146	0.184	0.084	<MDL	<MDL	<MDL	0.070[d]	<MDL
Codeine	<MDL	<MDL	<MDL	<MDL	<MDL	<MDL	0.136[d]	0.0960
Cotinine[c]	<MDL	<MDL	<MDL	<MDL	<MDL	0.014	0.036[d]	<MDL
Dehydronifedipine	<MDL	0.005	0.011	0.013[d]	0.013	0.011	0.057[d]	0.056
Diltiazem	0.042	0.042	0.060	0.053[d]	0.040	0.027	0.272[d]	0.150
1,7-Dimethylxanthine	<MDL	<MDL	<MDL	0.229[d]	<MDL	<MDL	<MDL	<MDL
Diphenhydramine	0.053	0.060	0.084	0.086[d]	0.219	0.191	0.352[d]	0.270
Erythromycin[b]	0.093	0.147	<MDL	<MDL	<MDL	<MDL	<MDL	<MDL
Fluoxetine	**<MDL**	**<MDL**	**<MDL**	**<MDL**	**<MDL**	**<MDL**	**<MDL**	**<MDL**
Furosemide	<MDL	<MDL	<MDL	<MDL	<MDL	<MDL	<MDL	<MDL
Gemfibrozil	<MDL	<MDL	<MDL	<MDL	<MDL	<MDL	<MDL	<MDL
Ibuprofen[b]	<MDL	<MDL	<MDL	<MDL	<MDL	<MDL	<MDL	<MDL
Metformin	<MDL	<MDL	<MDL	<MDL	<MDL	<MDL	<MDL	<MDL
Miconazole	<MDL	<MDL	<MDL	<MDL	<MDL	<MDL	<MDL	<MDL
Ranitidine	0.049	0.059	<MDL	<MDL	<MDL	<MDL	<MDL	<MDL
Sulfamethoxazole[b]	<MDL	<MDL	0.630	0.702[d]	<MDL	<MDL	<MDL	<MDL
Thiabendazole	<MDL	<MDL	<MDL	<MDL	<MDL	<MDL	<MDL	<MDL
Trimethoprim[b]	0.113	0.112	<MDL	<MDL	0.043	0.037	<MDL	<MDL
Warfarin	<MDL	<MDL	<MDL	<MDL	<MDL	<MDL	<MDL	<MDL

[a] Replicate samples.

[b] Secondary method of analysis for this analyte (see table 14 for preferred method of analysis).

[c] Preferred method of analysis for this analyte (see table 13 for secondary method of analysis).

[d] Internal standard response low.

Table 13. Concentrations of selected organic wastewater compounds and dissolved organic carbon in effluent from municipal wastewater-treatment facilities, before and after disinfection, in the Tar and Cape Fear River basins, North Carolina, May–July 2005

[UV, ultraviolet; µg/L, microgram per liter; <, less than; PAH, polycyclic aromatic hydrocarbon; NA, not analyzed; analytes with known or suspected hormonal activity are shown in **bold** type; the method of analysis for data presented in this table corresponds to that described in Zaugg and others (2002)]

Site identifier (table 1; figs. 2, 3)	Tar-WW01		Tar-WW03		CF-WW03		CF-WW07	
Disinfection status	before UV irradiation[a]	after UV irradiation	before chlorination	after chlorination	before UV irradiation	after UV irradiation	before chlorination	after chlorination
Date sample collected	05/06/05		07/22/05		06/24/05		07/14/05	
Analyte (µg/L)								
Detergent components and degradates								
4-Cumylphenol	<1.0	<1.0	<1.0	<1.0	<1.0	<1.0	<1.0	<1.0
p-Nonylphenol (total)	<5.0	<5.0	0.6[b]	0.7[b]	<5.0	<5.0	0.6	<5.0
Nonylphenol diethoxylates (NP2EO)	<5.0	<5.0	1.4[b]	1.1[b]	<5.0	<5.0	0.51	<5.0
4-*n*-Octylphenol	<1.0	<1.0	<1.0	<1.0	<1.0	<1.0	<1.0	<1.0
4-*t*-Octylphenol	<1.0	<1.0	<1.0	<1.0	<1.0	<1.0	<1.0	<1.0
4-*t*-Octylphenol monoethoxylates (OP1EO)	<1.0	<1.0	<1.0	<1.0	<1.0	<1.0	<1.0	<1.0
4-*t*-Octylphenol diethoxylates (OP2EO)	<1.0	<1.0	<1.0[c]	<1.0[c]	<1.0	<1.0	<1.0	<1.0
Flame retardants								
Tributyl phosphate	<0.5	<0.5	0.15[b]	0.14[b]	<0.5	<0.5	0.07[b]	0.07[b]
Tri(2-chloroethyl) phosphate	0.2[b]	0.2[b]	0.1[b]	0.2[b]	2.7	2.9	0.6	0.6
Tri(dichloroisopropyl) phosphate	0.48[b]	0.5	0.40[b]	0.39[b]	0.73	0.81	0.51	0.55
Triphenyl phosphate	0.03[b]	<0.5	0.04[b]	0.05[b]	<0.5	<0.5	<0.5	<0.5
Fragrances								
Acetophenone	<0.5	<0.5	<0.5	<0.5	<0.5	<0.5	<0.5	<0.5
Benzophenone	0.03[b]	0.06[b]	0.08[b]	0.12[b]	0.07[b]	0.13[b]	0.08[b]	0.09[b]
1,3,4,6,7,8-Hexahydro-4,6,6,7,8,8-hexamethylcyclopenta-γ-2-benzopyran (HHCB)	3.4	3.1	1.0	1.0	0.48[b]	0.58	1.1	1.2
Indole	<0.5	<0.5	<0.5	<0.5	<0.5	<0.5	<0.5	<0.5
3-Methyl-1H-indole (skatole)	<1.0	0.02[b]	0.04[b]	0.05[b]	0.04[b]	0.03[b]	<1.0	<1.0
Isoborneol	<0.5	<0.5	<0.5	<0.5	<0.5	<0.5	<0.5	<0.5
Menthol	<0.5	<0.5	<0.5	<0.5	<0.5	<0.5	<0.5	<0.5
Methyl salicylate	<0.5	<0.5	<0.5	<0.5	<0.5	<0.5	<0.5	<0.5
7-Acetyl-1,1,3,4,4,6-hexamethyl-1,2,3,4-tetrahydronaphthalene (AHTN)	1.1	0.84	0.18[b]	0.17[b]	0.08[b]	<0.5	0.28[b]	0.31[b]
PAHs, fossil fuel components, combustion byproducts								
Anthracene	<0.5	<0.5	<0.5	<0.5	<0.5	<0.5	<0.5	<0.5
Anthraquinone	<0.5	<0.5	0.06[b]	0.06[b]	<0.5	<0.5	<0.5	<0.5
p-Cresol	<1.0	<1.0	0.06[b]	0.1[b]	0.1[b]	0.05[b]	0.05[b]	0.03[b]
Fluoranthene	<0.5	<0.5	<0.5	<0.5	<0.5	<0.5	<0.5	<0.5

Table 13. Concentrations of selected organic wastewater compounds and dissolved organic carbon in effluent from municipal wastewater-treatment facilities, before and after disinfection, in the Tar and Cape Fear River basins, North Carolina, May–July 2005.—Continued

[UV, ultraviolet; µg/L, microgram per liter; <, less than; PAH, polycyclic aromatic hydrocarbon; NA, not analyzed; analytes with known or suspected hormonal activity are shown in **bold** type; the method of analysis for data presented in this table corresponds to that described in Zaugg and others (2002)]

Site identifier (table 1; figs. 2, 3)	Tar-WW01		Tar-WW03		CF-WW03		CF-WW07	
Disinfection status	before UV irradiation[a]	after UV irradiation[a]	before chlorination	after chlorination	before UV irradiation	after UV irradiation	before chlorination	after chlorination
Date sample collected	05/06/05		07/22/05		06/24/05		07/14/05	
Analyte (µg/L)								
Naphthalene	<0.5	<0.5	<0.5	<0.5	<0.5	<0.5	<0.5	<0.5
1-Methylnaphthalene	<0.5	<0.5	<0.5	<0.5	<0.5	<0.5	<0.5	<0.5
2-Methylnaphthalene	<0.5	<0.5	<0.5	<0.5	<0.5	<0.5	<0.5	<0.5
2,6-Dimethylnaphthalene	<0.5	<0.5	<0.5	<0.5	<0.5	<0.5	<0.5	<0.5
Phenanthrene	<0.5	<0.5	<0.5	<0.5	<0.5	<0.5	<0.5	<0.5
Pyrene	**<0.5**	**<0.5**	**<0.5**	**<0.5**	**<0.5**	**<0.5**	**<0.5**	**<0.5**
Benzo[a]pyrene	**<0.5**	**<0.5**	**<0.5**	**<0.5**	**<0.5**	**<0.5**	**<0.5**	**<0.5**
Pesticides								
Bromacil	**<0.5**	**<0.5**	**<0.5**	**<0.5**	**<0.5**	**<0.5**	**<0.5**	**<0.5**
Carbaryl	**<1.0**	**<1.0**	**0.1[b]**	**0.1[b]**	**<1.0**	**<1.0**	**1.2[b]**	**1.3[b]**
Carbazole	<0.5	<0.5	<0.5	<0.5	<0.5	<0.5	<0.5	<0.5
Chlorpyrifos	**<0.5**	**<0.5**	**<0.5**	**<0.5**	**<0.5**	**<0.5**	**<0.5**	**<0.5**
Diazinon	**<0.5**	**<0.5**	**<0.5**	**<0.5**	**<0.5**	**<0.5**	**<0.5**	**<0.5**
d-Limonene	<0.5	<0.5	<0.5	<0.5	<0.5	<0.5	<0.5	<0.5
Metalaxyl	<0.5	<0.5	<0.5	<0.5	<0.5	<0.5	<0.5	<0.5
Metolachlor	<0.5	<0.5	0.06[b]	0.06[b]	0.07[b]	0.08[b]	0.21[b]	0.22[b]
Pentachlorophenol	**NA**	**NA**	**0.1[b]**	**0.08[b]**	**<2.0**	**<2.0**	**<2.0**	**<2.0**
Prometon	0.14[b]	0.13[b]	<0.5	<0.5	<0.5	<0.5	<0.5	<0.5
Pharmaceutical compounds and metabolites								
Caffeine[d]	0.09[b]	0.08[b]	0.10[b]	0.24[b]	0.04[b]	0.05[b]	<0.5	<0.5
Cotinine[d]	<1.0	<1.0	<1.0	<1.0	<1.0	<1.0	<1.0	<1.0
Isoquinoline	<0.5	<0.5	<0.5	<0.5	<0.5	<0.5	<0.5	<0.5
Plasticizers								
Bisphenol A	**0.2[b]**	**0.3[b]**	**<1.0**	**<1.0**	**<1.0**	**<1.0**	**<1.0**	**<1.0**
Camphor	<0.5	<0.5	<0.5	<0.5	<0.5	<0.5	<0.5	<0.5
Triethyl citrate (ethyl citrate)	0.07[b]	0.08[b]	0.15[b]	0.16[b]	0.11[b]	0.13[b]	<0.5	<0.5
Tri(2-butoxyethyl) phosphate	<0.5	<0.5	0.33[b]	0.65	1.9	2.0	<0.5	<0.5
Solvents								
Isophorone	<0.5	<0.5	<0.5	<0.5	<0.5	<0.5	<0.5	<0.5
Isopropylbenzene (cumene)	<0.5	<0.5	<0.5	<0.5	<0.5	<0.5	<0.5	<0.5
Tetrachloroethylene (PCE)	<0.5	<0.5	0.05[b]	0.04[b]	<0.5	<0.5	<0.5	<0.5

Table 13. Concentrations of selected organic wastewater compounds and dissolved organic carbon in effluent from municipal wastewater-treatment facilities, before and after disinfection, in the Tar and Cape Fear River basins, North Carolina, May–July 2005.—Continued

[UV, ultraviolet; μg/L, microgram per liter; <, less than; PAH, polycyclic aromatic hydrocarbon; NA, not analyzed; analytes with known or suspected hormonal activity are shown in **bold** type; the method of analysis for data presented in this table corresponds to that described in Zaugg and others (2002)]

Site identifier (table 1; figs. 2, 3) Disinfection status	Tar -WW01		Tar-WW03		CF-WW03		CF-WW07	
	before UV irradiation[a]	after UV irradiation	before chlorination	after chlorination	before UV irradiation	after UV irradiation	before chlorination	after chlorination
Date sample collected	05/06/05		07/22/05		06/24/05		07/14/05	
Analyte (μg/L)								
Biogenic sterols								
Cholesterol	<2.0	<2.0	0.8[b]	<2.0	0.7[b]	0.6[b]	<2.0	<2.0
3-β-Coprostanol	<2.0	<2.0	0.5[b]	<2.0	<2.0	<2.0	<2.0	<2.0
β-Sitosterol	**<2.0**	**<2.0**	**0.7[b]**	**<2.0**	**<2.0**	**<2.0**	**<2.0**	**<2.0**
β-Stigmastanol	<2.0	<2.0	0.7[b]	<2.0	<2.0	<2.0	<2.0	<2.0
Miscellaneous compounds and dissolved organic carbon								
3-/-Butyl-4-hydroxyanisole (BHA)	**<5.0**	**<5.0**	**<5.0**	**<5.0**	**<5.0**	**<5.0**	**<5.0**	**<5.0**
1,4-Dichlorobenzene	**0.04[b]**	**<0.5**	**0.20[b]**	**0.16[b]**	**0.09[b]**	**0.09[b]**	**0.04[b]**	**0.03[b]**
5-Methyl-1H-benzotriazole	<2.0	<2.0	<2.0	<2.0	<2.0	<2.0	<2.0	<2.0
Bromoform	<0.5	<0.5	<0.5	<0.5	0.18[b]	0.17[b]	<0.5	0.07[b]
Triclosan	**0.07[b]**	**<1.0**	**0.2[b]**	**0.2[b]**	**<1.0**	**<1.0**	**<1.0**	**0.2[b]**
Dissolved organic carbon[e]	1,500	NA	1,100	41	1,000		1,000	

[a] Replicate samples.

[b] Estimated concentration (analyte detected at a concentration outside the range of calibration).

[c] Analyte detected in sample at a concentration less than 10 times that in an associated laboratory or field blank.

[d] Secondary method of analysis for this analyte (see table 12 for preferred method of analysis).

[e] Concentration of dissolved organic carbon is expressed in milligrams per liter.

Table 14. Concentrations of selected antibiotics, antibiotic metabolites, and pharmaceutical compounds in effluent from municipal wastewater-treatment facilities, before and after disinfection, in the Tar and Cape Fear River basins, North Carolina, May–July 2005

[UV, ultraviolet; µg/L, microgram per liter; <, less than; the method of analysis for data presented in this table corresponds to that described in Meyer and others (2007)]

Site identifier (table 1; figs. 2, 3)	Tar River Basin				Cape Fear River Basin			
	Tar-WW01		Tar-WW03		CF-WW03		CF-WW06	
Disinfection status	before UV disinfection	after UV disinfection	before chlorination	after chlorination	before UV disinfection	after UV disinfection	before chlorination	after chlorination
Date sample collected	05/06/05		07/22/05		06/24/05		07/14/05	
Analyte (µg/L)								
Macrolide antibiotics and metabolites								
Azithromycin[a]	0.140	0.017	0.097	0.241	0.434	0.194	0.365	0.563
Erythromycin[a]	0.008	0.015	<0.008	<0.008	<0.008	<0.008	<0.008	<0.008
Erythromycin-H$_2$O[b]	0.042	0.102	0.021	0.025	<0.005	0.011	0.036	0.038
Roxithromycin	<0.005	<0.005	<0.005	<0.005	<0.005	<0.005	<0.005	<0.005
Tylosin	<0.005	<0.005	<0.005	<0.005	<0.005	<0.005	<0.005	<0.005
Virginiamycin	<0.005	<0.005	<0.005	<0.005	<0.005	<0.005	<0.005	<0.005
Fluoroquinolone antibiotics								
Ciprofloxacin	0.044	0.025	0.008	0.008	0.087	0.066	0.120	0.024
Enrofloxacin	<0.005	<0.005	<0.005	<0.005	<0.005	<0.005	<0.005	<0.005
Lomefloxacin	<0.005	<0.005	<0.005	<0.005	<0.005	<0.005	<0.005	<0.005
Norfloxacin	<0.005	<0.005	<0.005	<0.005	0.015	0.015	<0.005	<0.005
Ofloxacin	0.100	0.051	0.060	0.018	0.103	0.104	0.188	0.067
Sarafloxacin	<0.005	<0.010	<0.005	<0.005	<0.005	<0.005	<0.005	<0.005
Sulfonamide antibiotics								
Sulfachloropyridazine	<0.005	<0.005	<0.005	<0.005	<0.005	<0.005	<0.005	<0.005
Sulfadiazine	<0.050	<0.050	<0.005	<0.005	<0.005	<0.005	<0.005	<0.005
Sulfadimethoxine	<0.005	<0.005	<0.005	<0.005	<0.005	<0.005	<0.005	<0.005
Sulfamethoxazole[a]	0.695	0.606	0.053	<0.005	0.031	0.080	0.580	0.417
Sulfamethazine	<0.005	<0.050	<0.005	<0.005	<0.005	<0.005	<0.005	<0.005
Sulfathiazole	<0.020	<0.020	<0.020	<0.020	<0.020	<0.020	<0.020	<0.020
Tetracycline antibiotics and metabolites								
Chlortetracycline	<0.010	<0.010	<0.010	<0.010	<0.010	<0.010	<0.010	<0.010
Epi-chlortetracycline[b]	<0.010	<0.010	<0.010	<0.010	<0.010	<0.010	<0.010	<0.010
Epi-iso-chlortetracycline[b]	<0.010	<0.010	<0.010	<0.010	<0.010	<0.010	<0.010	<0.010
Iso-chlortetracycline[b]	<0.010	<0.010	<0.010	<0.010	<0.010	<0.010	<0.010	<0.010
Doxycycline	<0.010	<0.010	<0.010	<0.010	<0.010	<0.010	<0.010	<0.010
Oxytetracycline	<0.010	<0.010	<0.010	<0.010	<0.010	<0.010	<0.010	<0.010
Epi-oxytetracycline[b]	<0.010	<0.010	<0.010	<0.010	<0.010	<0.010	<0.010	<0.010
Tetracycline	<0.010	<0.010	<0.010	<0.010	<0.010	<0.010	<0.010	<0.010
Epi-tetracycline[b]	<0.010	<0.010	<0.010	<0.010	<0.010	<0.010	<0.010	<0.010

Table 14. Concentrations of selected antibiotics, antibiotic metabolites, and pharmaceutical compounds in effluent from municipal wastewater-treatment facilities, before and after disinfection, in the Tar and Cape Fear River basins, North Carolina, May–July 2005.—Continued

[UV, ultraviolet; µg/L, microgram per liter; <, less than; the method of analysis for data presented in this table corresponds to that described in Meyer and others (2007)]

Site identifier (table 1: figs. 2, 3)	Tar River Basin				Cape Fear River Basin			
	Tar-WW01		Tar-WW03		CF-WW03		CF-WW06	
Disinfection status	before UV disinfection	after UV disinfection	before chlorination	after chlorination	before UV disinfection	after UV disinfection	before chlorination	after chlorination
Date sample collected	05/06/05		07/22/05		06/24/05		07/14/05	
Analyte (µg/L)								
Miscellaneous antibiotics								
Lincomycin	<0.005	<0.005	0.499	0.055	<0.005	<0.005	<0.005	<0.005
Chloramphenicol	<0.010	<0.010	<0.010	<0.010	<0.010	<0.010	<0.010	<0.010
Ormetoprim	<0.005	<0.005	<0.005	<0.005	<0.005	<0.005	<0.005	<0.005
Trimethoprim[a]	0.172	0.138	0.031	0.036	0.061	0.085	0.024	0.018
Pharmaceutical compounds								
Carbamazepine[a]	0.323	0.254	0.284	0.243	0.832	0.856	0.360	0.396
Ibuprofen[a]	<0.050	<0.050	<0.050	<0.050	<0.050	<0.050	<0.050	<0.050

[a] Preferred method of analysis for this analyte (see table 12 for secondary method of analysis).

[b] Antibiotic metabolite.

Table 15. Concentrations of selected pharmaceutical compounds and metabolites in water samples at various stages of treatment from municipal drinking-water treatment facilities in the Tar River Basin, North Carolina, February and July 2005.

[μg/L, microgram per liter; <, less than; MDL, method detection limit; analytes with known or suspected hormonal activity are shown in **bold** type; the method of analysis for data presented in this table is described in Cahill and others (2004)]

Site identifier (table 2; fig. 2)	Tar-DW02			Tar-DW03					
Treatment stage	Raw water	Settled water	Finished water	Raw water	Impounded water	Settled ozonation	Filtered	Clearwell	Finished water (chlorinated)
Date sample collected	02/11/05			07/12/05					
Analyte [μg/L]									
Acetaminophen	<MDL	<MDL	<MDL	<MDL	<MDL	<MDL	0.014	<MDL	<MDL
Albuterol	<MDL	<MDL	<MDL	<MDL	<MDL	<MDL	<MDL	<MDL	<MDL
Azithromycin[a,b]	<MDL	<MDL	<MDL	<MDL	<MDL	<MDL	<MDL	<MDL	<MDL
Caffeine[c]	<MDL	<MDL	<MDL	<MDL	<MDL	<MDL	0.016	<MDL	<MDL
Carbamazepine[a,b]	<MDL	<MDL	<MDL	0.0064	0.0058	0.0054	<MDL	<MDL	<MDL
Cimetidine	<MDL	<MDL	<MDL	<MDL	<MDL	<MDL	<MDL	<MDL	<MDL
Codeine	<MDL	<MDL	<MDL	<MDL	<MDL	<MDL	<MDL	<MDL	<MDL
Cotinine[c]	<MDL	<MDL	<MDL	0.005	0.006	0.006	<MDL	0.003	<MDL
Dehydronifedipine	<MDL	<MDL	<MDL	<MDL	<MDL	<MDL	<MDL	<MDL	<MDL
Diltiazem	<MDL	<MDL	<MDL	<MDL	<MDL	<MDL	<MDL	<MDL	<MDL
1,7-Dimethylxanthine	<MDL	<MDL	<MDL	<MDL	<MDL	<MDL	<MDL	0.021	<MDL
Diphenhydramine[a]	0.006[d]	<MDL	<MDL	0.004[d]	0.005[d]	0.005[d]	0.016	<MDL	0.012
Erythromycin[a,b]	<MDL	<MDL	<MDL	<MDL	<MDL	<MDL	<MDL	<MDL	<MDL
Fluoxetine	**<MDL**	**<MDL**	**<MDL**	**<MDL**	**<MDL**	**<MDL**	**<MDL**	**<MDL**	**<MDL**
Furosemide	<MDL	<MDL	<MDL	<MDL	<MDL	<MDL	<MDL	<MDL	<MDL
Gemfibrozil	<MDL	<MDL	<MDL	<MDL	<MDL	<MDL	<MDL	<MDL	<MDL
Ibuprofen[b]	<MDL	<MDL	<MDL	<MDL	<MDL	<MDL	<MDL	<MDL	<MDL
Metformin	<MDL	<MDL	<MDL	<MDL	<MDL	<MDL	<MDL	<MDL	<MDL
Miconazole[a]	<MDL	<MDL	<MDL	<MDL	<MDL	<MDL	<MDL	<MDL	<MDL
Ranitidine	<MDL	<MDL	<MDL	<MDL	<MDL	<MDL	<MDL	<MDL	<MDL
Sulfamethoxazole[b]	<MDL	<MDL	<MDL	<MDL	<MDL	<MDL	<MDL	<MDL	<MDL
Thiabendazole[a]	<MDL	<MDL	<MDL	<MDL	<MDL	<MDL	<MDL	<MDL	<MDL
Trimethoprim[b]	<MDL	<MDL	<MDL	<MDL	<MDL	<MDL	<MDL	<MDL	<MDL
Warfarin[b]	<MDL	<MDL	<MDL	<MDL	<MDL	<MDL	<MDL	<MDL	<MDL

[a] Method detection limit not established at time of analysis.

[b] Secondary method of analysis for this analyte (see table 19 for preferred method of analysis).

[c] Preferred method of analysis for this analyte (see table 17 for secondary method of analysis).

[d] Estimated concentration (analyte detected at a concentration outside the range of calibration).

Table 16. Concentrations of selected pharmaceutical compounds and metabolites in water samples at various stages of treatment from municipal drinking-water treatment facilities in the Cape Fear River basin, North Carolina, July–August 2005.

[µg/L, microgram per liter; <, less than; MDL, method detection limit; analytes with known or suspected hormonal activity are shown in **bold** type; the method of analysis for data presented in this table is described in Cahill and others (2004)]

Site identifier (table 2; fig. 3)	CF-DW02		CF-DW06				
Treatment stage	Raw water	Finished water	Raw water	Impounded	Settled	Clearwell	Finished water
Date sample collected	08/04/05		07/14/05				
Analyte (µg/L)							
Acetaminophen	<MDL	<MDL	0.014	<MDL	<MDL	<MDL	<MDL
Albuterol	<MDL	<MDL	<MDL	<MDL	<MDL	<MDL	<MDL
Azithromycin[a]	<MDL	<MDL	<MDL	<MDL	<MDL	<MDL	<MDL
Caffeine[b]	0.031	<MDL	0.073	<MDL[c]	<MDL[c]	<MDL	<MDL
Carbamazepine[a]	0.014	0.009	<MDL	<MDL	<MDL	<MDL	<MDL
Cimetidine	<MDL	<MDL	<MDL	<MDL	<MDL	<MDL	<MDL
Codeine	<MDL	<MDL	<MDL	<MDL	<MDL	<MDL	<MDL
Cotinine[b]	0.011	0.009	0.010	0.009	0.008	0.008	0.008
Dehydronifedipine	<MDL	<MDL	<MDL	<MDL	<MDL	<MDL	<MDL
Diltiazem	<MDL	<MDL	<MDL	<MDL	<MDL	<MDL	<MDL
1,7-Dimethylxanthine	<MDL	<MDL	<MDL	<MDL	<MDL	<MDL	<MDL
Diphenhydramine	<MDL	<MDL	<MDL	<MDL	<MDL	<MDL[c]	<MDL[c]
Erythromycin[a]	<MDL	<MDL	<MDL	<MDL	<MDL	<MDL	<MDL
Fluoxetine	**<MDL**	**<MDL**	**<MDL**	**<MDL**	**<MDL**	**<MDL**	**<MDL**
Furosemide	<MDL	<MDL	<MDL	<MDL	<MDL	<MDL	<MDL
Gemfibrozil	<MDL	<MDL	<MDL	<MDL	<MDL	<MDL	<MDL
Ibuprofen[a]	<MDL	<MDL	<MDL	<MDL	<MDL	<MDL	<MDL
Metformin	<MDL	<MDL	<MDL	<MDL	<MDL	<MDL	<MDL
Miconazole	<MDL	<MDL	<MDL	<MDL	<MDL	<MDL	<MDL
Ranitidine	<MDL	<MDL	<MDL	<MDL	<MDL	<MDL	<MDL
Sulfamethoxazole[a]	<MDL	<MDL	<MDL	<MDL	<MDL	<MDL	<MDL
Thiabendazole	<MDL	<MDL	<MDL	<MDL	<MDL	<MDL	<MDL
Trimethoprim[a]	<MDL	<MDL	<MDL	<MDL	<MDL	<MDL	<MDL
Warfarin	<MDL	<MDL	<MDL	<MDL	<MDL	<MDL	<MDL

Table 16. Concentrations of selected pharmaceutical compounds and metabolites in water samples at various stages of treatment from municipal drinking-water treatment facilities in the Cape Fear River basin, North Carolina, July–August 2005.—Continued

[µg/L, microgram per liter; <, less than; MDL, method detection limit; analytes with known or suspected hormonal activity are shown in **bold** type; the method of analysis for data presented in this table is described in Cahill and others (2004)]

Site identifier (table 2; fig. 3)	CF-DW07					
Treatment stage	Raw water[d]	Raw water[d]	Preozonation	Settled	Clarification and ozonation (prefiltration)	Finished (chlorination)
Date sample collected	07/21/05					
Analyte (µg/L)						
Acetaminophen	<MDL	<MDL	<MDL	<MDL	<MDL	<MDL
Albuterol	<MDL	<MDL	<MDL	<MDL	<MDL	<MDL
Azithromycin[a]	<MDL	<MDL	<MDL	<MDL	<MDL	<MDL
Caffeine[b]	<MDL	<MDL	<MDL	<MDL	<MDL	<MDL
Carbamazepine[a]	0.009	0.012	0.008	<MDL	<MDL	<MDL
Cimetidine	<MDL	<MDL	<MDL	<MDL	<MDL	<MDL
Codeine	<MDL	<MDL	<MDL	<MDL	<MDL	<MDL
Cotinine[b]	0.010	0.011	0.009	0.008	0.006[e]	0.004[e]
Dehydronifedipine	<MDL	<MDL	<MDL	<MDL	<MDL	<MDL
Diltiazem	<MDL	<MDL	<MDL	<MDL	<MDL	<MDL
1,7-Dimethylxanthine	<MDL	<MDL	<MDL	<MDL	<MDL	<MDL
Diphenhydramine	<MDL[c]	<MDL	<MDL[c]	<MDL	<MDL	<MDL[c]
Erythromycin[a]	<MDL	<MDL	<MDL	<MDL	<MDL	<MDL
Fluoxetine	**<MDL**	**<MDL**	**<MDL**	**<MDL**	**<MDL**	**<MDL**
Furosemide	<MDL	<MDL	<MDL	<MDL	<MDL	<MDL
Gemfibrozil	<MDL	<MDL	<MDL	<MDL	<MDL	<MDL
Ibuprofen[a]	<MDL	<MDL	<MDL	<MDL	<MDL	<MDL
Metformin	<MDL	<MDL	<MDL	<MDL	<MDL	<MDL
Miconazole	<MDL	<MDL	<MDL	<MDL	<MDL	<MDL
Ranitidine	<MDL	<MDL	<MDL	<MDL	<MDL	<MDL
Sulfamethoxazole[a]	<MDL	<MDL	<MDL	<MDL	<MDL	<MDL
Thiabendazole	<MDL	<MDL	<MDL	<MDL	<MDL	<MDL
Trimethoprim[a]	<MDL	<MDL	<MDL	<MDL	<MDL	<MDL
Warfarin	<MDL	<MDL	<MDL	<MDL	<MDL	<MDL

[a] Secondary method of analysis for this analyte (see table 20 for preferred method of analysis).

[b] Preferred method of analysis for this analyte (see table 18 for secondary method of analysis).

[c] Compound detected in laboratory blank.

[d] Replicate samples.

[e] Estimated concentration (analyte detected at a concentration outside the range of calibration).

Table 17. Concentrations of selected organic wastewater compounds in water at various stages of treatment from municipal drinking-water treatment facilities in the Tar River basin, North Carolina, February and July 2005.

[µg/L, microgram per liter; <, less than; PAH, polycyclic aromatic hydrocarbon; NA, not analyzed; analytes with known or suspected hormonal activity are shown in **bold** type; the method of analysis for data presented in this table corresponds to that described in Zaugg and others (2002)]

Site identifier (table 2; fig. 2)	Tar-DW02			Tar-DW03					
Treatment stage	Raw	Settled	Finished	Raw	Impounded	Settled ozonation	Filtered	Clearwell	Finished (chlorination)
Date sample collected		02/11/05				07/12/05			
Analyte (µg/L)									
Detergent components and degradates									
4-cumylphenol	**<1.0**	**<1.0**	**<1.0**	**<1.0**	**<1.0**	**<1.0**	**<1.0**	**<1.0**	**<1.0**
***p*-Nonylphenol (total)**	**<5.0**	**<5.0**	**<5.0**	**<5.0**	**<5.0**	**<5.0**	**<5.0**	**<5.0**	**<5.0**
Nonylphenol diethoxylates (NP2EO)	**<5.0**	**<5.0**	**<5.0**	**<5.0**	**<5.0**	**<5.0**	**<5.0**	**<5.0**	**<5.0**
4-*n*-Octylphenol	**<1.0**	**<1.0**	**<1.0**	**<1.0**	**<1.0**	**<1.0**	**<1.0**	**<1.0**	**<1.0**
4-*t*-Octylphenol	**<1.0**	**<1.0**	**<1.0**	**<1.0**	**<1.0**	**<1.0**	**<1.0**	**<1.0**	**<1.0**
4-*t*-Octylphenol monoethoxylates (OP1EO)	**<1.0**	**<1.0**	**<1.0**	**<1.0**	**<1.0**	**<1.0**	**<1.0**	**<1.0**	**<1.0**
4-*t*-Octylphenol diethoxylates (OP2EO)	**<1.0**	**<1.0**	**<1.0**	**<1.0**	**<1.0**	**<1.0**	**<1.0**	**<1.0**	**<1.0**
Flame retardants									
Tributyl phosphate	<0.5	0.06[a]	0.06[a]	<0.5	<0.5	<0.5	<0.5	<0.5	<0.5
Tri(2-chloroethyl) phosphate	<0.5	<0.5	<0.5	<0.5	<0.5	<0.5	<0.5	<0.5	<0.5
Tri(dichloroisopropyl) phosphate	<0.5	<0.5	<0.5	0.04[a]	<0.5	<0.5	<0.5	<0.5	<0.5
Triphenyl phosphate	<0.5	<0.5	<0.5	<0.5	<0.5	<0.5	<0.5	<0.5	<0.5
Fragrances									
Acetophenone	<0.5	<0.5	<0.5	<0.5	<0.5	<0.5	<0.5	<0.5	<0.5
Benzophenone	**<0.5**	**<0.5**	**<0.5**	**<0.5**	**<0.5[b]**	**<0.5**	**<0.5**	**<0.5**	**<0.5**
1,3,4,6,7,8-Hexahydro-4,6,6,7,8,8-hexamethyl-cyclopenta-γ-2-benzopyran (HHCB)	<0.5	<0.5	<0.5	<0.5	<0.5	<0.5	<0.5	<0.5	<0.5
Indole	<0.5	<0.5	<0.5	<0.5	<0.5	<0.5	<0.5	<0.5	<0.5
3-Methyl-1H-indole (skatole)	<1.0	<1.0	<1.0	<1.0	<1.0	<1.0	<1.0	<1.0	<1.0
Isoborneol	<0.5	<0.5	<0.5	<0.5	<0.5	<0.5	<0.5	<0.5	<0.5
Menthol	<0.5	<0.5	<0.5	<0.5	<0.5	<0.5	<0.5	<0.5	<0.5
Methyl salicylate	<0.5	<0.5	<0.5	<0.5	<0.5	<0.5	<0.5	<0.5	<0.5
7-Acetyl-1,1,3,4,4,6-hexamethyl-1,2,3,4-tetrahydronaphthalene (AHTN)	**<0.5**	**<0.5**	**<0.5**	**0.01[a]**	**0.01[a]**	**<0.5**	**<0.5**	**<0.5**	**<0.5**
PAHs, fossil fuel components, and combustion byproducts									
Anthracene	<0.5	<0.5	<0.5	<0.5	<0.5	<0.5	<0.5	<0.5	<0.5
Anthraquinone	<0.5	<0.5	<0.5	<0.5	<0.5	<0.5	<0.5	<0.5	<0.5
p-Cresol	<1.0	<1.0	<1.0	<1.0	<1.0	<1.0	<1.0	<1.0	<1.0
Fluoranthene	<0.5	<0.5	<0.5	<0.5	<0.5	<0.5	<0.5	<0.5	<0.5
Naphthalene	<0.5	<0.5	<0.5	<0.5	<0.5	<0.5	<0.5	<0.5	<0.5
1-Methylnaphthalene	<0.5	<0.5	<0.5	<0.5	<0.5	<0.5	<0.5	<0.5	<0.5
2-Methylnaphthalene	<0.5	<0.5	<0.5	<0.5	<0.5	<0.5	<0.5	<0.5	<0.5

Table 17. Concentrations of selected organic wastewater compounds in water at various stages of treatment from municipal drinking-water treatment facilities in the Tar River basin, North Carolina, February and July 2005.—Continued

[μg/L, microgram per liter; <, less than; PAH, polycyclic aromatic hydrocarbon; NA, not analyzed; analytes with known or suspected hormonal activity are shown in **bold** type; the method of analysis for data presented in this table corresponds to that described in Zaugg and others (2002)]

Site identifier (table 2; fig. 2)	Tar-DW02			Tar-DW03					
Treatment stage	Raw	Settled	Finished	Raw	Impounded	Settled ozonation	Filtered	Clearwell	Finished (chlorination)
Date sample collected	02/11/05			07/12/05					
Analyte (μg/L)									
2,6-Dimethylnaphthalene	<0.5	<0.5	<0.5	<0.5	<0.5	<0.5	<0.5	<0.5	<0.5
Phenanthrene	<0.5	<0.5	<0.5	<0.5	<0.5	<0.5	<0.5	<0.5	<0.5
Pyrene	**<0.5**	**<0.5**	**<0.5**	**<0.5**	**<0.5**	**<0.5**	**<0.5**	**<0.5**	**<0.5**
Benzo[a]pyrene	**<0.5**	**<0.5**	**<0.5**	**<0.5**	**<0.5**	**<0.5**	**<0.5**	**<0.5**	**<0.5**
Pesticides									
Bromacil	**<0.5**	**<0.5**	**<0.5**	**<0.5**	**<0.5**	**<0.5**	**<0.5**	**<0.5**	**<0.5**
Carbaryl	**<1.0**	**<1.0**	**<1.0**	**<1.0**	**<1.0**	**<1.0**	**<1.0**	**<1.0**	**<1.0**
Carbazole	<0.5	<0.5	<0.5	<0.5	<0.5	<0.5	<0.5	<0.5	<0.5
Chlorpyrifos	**<0.5**	**<0.5**	**<0.5**	**<0.5**	**<0.5**	**<0.5**	**<0.5**	**<0.5**	**<0.5**
Diazinon	**<0.5**	**<0.5**	**<0.5**	**<0.5**	**<0.5**	**<0.5**	**<0.5**	**<0.5**	**<0.5**
d-Limonene	<0.5	<0.5	<0.5	<0.5	0.03[a]	<0.5	0.02[a]	0.05[a]	<0.5
Metalaxyl	<0.5	<0.5	<0.5	<0.5	<0.5	<0.5	<0.5	<0.5	<0.5
Metolachlor	<0.5	<0.5	<0.5	0.07[a]	0.15[a]	0.17[a]	<0.5	<0.5	<0.5
Pentachlorophenol	**<2.0**	**<2.0**	**<2.0**	NA	NA	NA	NA	NA	NA
Prometon	<0.5	<0.5	<0.5	0.05[a]	0.05[a]	0.07[a]	<0.5	<0.5	<0.5
Pharmaceuticals									
Caffeine[c]	<0.5	<0.5	<0.5	0.01[a]	0.02[a]	0.04[a]	<0.5	<0.5	<0.5
Cotinine[c]	<1.0	<1.0	<1.0	<1.0	<1.0	<1.0	<1.0	<1.0	<1.0
Isoquinoline	<0.5	<0.5	<0.5	<0.5	<0.5	<0.5	<0.5	<0.5	<0.5
Plasticizers									
Bisphenol A	**<1.0**	**<1.0**	**<1.0**	**<0.5**	NA	NA	NA	NA	NA
Camphor	<0.5	<0.5	<0.5	<0.5	<0.5	<0.5	<0.5	<0.5	<0.5
Triethyl citrate (ethyl citrate)	<0.5	<0.5	<0.5	<0.5	<0.5	<0.5	<0.5	<0.5	<0.5
Tri(2-butoxyethyl) phosphate	<0.5	<0.5	<0.5	<0.5	<0.5	<0.5	<0.5	<0.5	<0.5
Solvents									
Isophorone	<0.5	<0.5	<0.5	<0.5	<0.5	<0.5	<0.5	<0.5	<0.5
Isopropylbenzene (cumene)	<0.5	<0.5	<0.5	<0.5	<0.5	<0.5	<0.5	<0.5	<0.5
Tetrachloroethylene (PCE)	<0.5	<0.5	<0.5	<0.5	0.01[a]	<0.5	<0.5	<0.5	0.02[a]
Biogenic sterols									
Cholesterol	0.5[a]	0.6[a]	<2.0	0.4[a]	0.4[a]	<2.0	<2.0	<2.0	<2.0
3-β-Coprostanol	<2.0	<2.0	<2.0	<2.0	<2.0	<2.0	<2.0	<2.0	<2.0
β-Sitosterol	**<2.0**	**<2.0**	**<2.0**	**<2.0**	**<2.0**	**<2.0**	**<2.0**	**<2.0**	**<2.0**
β-Stigmastanol	<2.0	<2.0	<2.0	<2.0	<2.0	<2.0	<2.0	<2.0	<2.0

Table 17. Concentrations of selected organic wastewater compounds in water at various stages of treatment from municipal drinking-water treatment facilities in the Tar River basin, North Carolina, February and July 2005.—Continued

[µg/L, microgram per liter; <, less than; PAH, polycyclic aromatic hydrocarbon; NA, not analyzed; analytes with known or suspected hormonal activity are shown in **bold** type; the method of analysis for data presented in this table corresponds to that described in Zaugg and others (2002)]

Site identifier (table 2; fig. 2)	Tar-DW02			Tar-DW03					
Treatment stage	Raw	Settled	Finished	Raw	Impounded	Settled ozonation	Filtered	Clearwell	Finished (chlorination)
Date sample collected	02/11/05			07/12/05					
Analyte (µg/L)									
Miscellaneous compounds and dissolved organic carbon									
3-*t*-Butyl-4-hydroxyanisole (BHA)	**<5.0**	**<5.0**	**<5.0**	**<5.0**	**<5.0**	**<5.0**	**<5.0**	**<5.0**	**<5.0**
1,4-dichlorobenzene	**<0.5**	**<0.5**	**<0.5**	**<0.5**	**<0.5**	**<0.5**	**<0.5**	**<0.5**	**<0.5**
5-Methyl-1H-benzotriazole	<2.0	<2.0	<2.0	NA	NA	NA	NA	NA	NA
Bromoform	<0.5	<0.5	26.0[a]	0.03[a]	<0.5	0.5	0.13[a]	0.13[a]	0.15[a]
Triclosan	**<1.0**	**<1.0**	**<1.0**	**<1.0**	**<1.0**	**<1.0**	**<1.0**	**<1.0**	**<1.0**
Dissolved organic carbon[d]	490	18	5.5	960	130	85	16	6.6	2.9

[a] Estimated concentration (analyte detected at concentration outside of the range of calibration).

[b] Analyte detected in sample at a concentration less than 10 times that in an associated laboratory or field blank.

[c] Secondary method of analysis for this analyte (see table 15 for preferred method of analysis).

[d] Concentration of dissolved organic carbon expressed in milligrams per liter.

Table 18. Concentrations of selected organic wastewater compounds in samples of water at various stages of treatment from municipal drinking-water treatment facilities in the Cape Fear River basin, North Carolina, July and August 2005.

[µg/L, microgram per liter; <, less than; PAH, polycyclic aromatic hydrocarbon; NA, not analyzed; analytes with known or suspected hormonal activity are shown in **bold** type; the method of analysis for data presented in this table corresponds to that described in Zaugg and others (2002)]

Site identifier (table 2; fig. 3)	CF-DW02			CF-DW06				
Treatment stage	Raw[a]	Raw[a]	Finished (chlorination)	Raw	Impounded	Settled	Clarified	Finished (chlorination)
Date sample collected	08/04/05			07/14/05				
Analyte (µg/L)								
Detergent components and degrades								
4-Cumylphenol	<1.0	<1.0	<1.0	<1.0	<1.0	<1.0	<1.0	<1.0
***p*-Nonylphenol (total)**	<5.0	<5.0	<5.0	<5.0	<5.0	<5.0	<5.0	<5.0
Nonylphenol diethoxylates (NP2EO)	<5.0	<5.0	<5.0	<5.0	<5.0	<5.0	<5.0[b]	<5.0
4-*n*-Octylphenol	<1.0	<1.0	<1.0	<1.0	<1.0	<1.0	<1.0	<1.0
4-*t*-Octylphenol	<1.0	<1.0	<1.0	<1.0	<1.0	<1.0	<1.0	<1.0
4-*t*-Octylphenol monoethoxylates (OP1EO)	<1.0	<1.0	<1.0	<1.0	<1.0	<1.0	<1.0	<1.0
4-*t*-Octylphenol diethoxylates (OP2EO)	<1.0[b]	<1.0	<1.0[b]	<1.0	<1.0	<1.0	<1.0[b]	<1.0
Flame retardants								
Tributyl phosphate	<0.5	0.06[c]	<0.5	<0.5[b]	<0.5[b]	<0.5[b]	<0.5[b]	<0.5[b]
Tri(2-chloroethyl) phosphate	<0.5	<0.5	<0.5	0.3[c]	0.3[c]	0.3[c]	0.3[c]	0.4[c]
Tri(dichloroisopropyl) phosphate	0.07[c]	<0.5	0.08[c]	<0.5[b]	<0.5[b]	<0.5[b]	<0.5[b]	<0.5[b]
Triphenyl phosphate	<0.5	<0.5	<0.5	<0.5	<0.5	<0.5	<0.5	<0.5
Fragrances								
Acetophenone	<0.5	<0.5	<0.5	<0.5	<0.5	<0.5	<0.5	<0.5
Benzophenone	<0.5	<0.5	<0.5	<0.5	<0.5	<0.5	<0.5[b]	<0.5[b]
1,3,4,6,7,8-Hexahydro-4,6,6,7,8,8-hexamethyl-cyclopenta-γ-2-benzopyran (HHCB)	<0.5	<0.5	<0.5	<0.5	<0.5	<0.5	<0.5	<0.5
Indole	0.02[c]	<0.5	<0.5	<0.5	0.02[c]	<0.5	<0.5	<0.5
3-Methyl-1H-indole (skatole)	<1.0	<1.0	<1.0	<1.0	<1.0	<1.0	<1.0	<1.0
Isoborneol	<0.5	<0.5	<0.5	<0.5	<0.5	<0.5	<0.5	<0.5
Menthol	<0.5	<0.5	<0.5	<0.5	<0.5	<0.5	<0.5	<0.5
Methyl salicylate	<0.5	<0.5	<0.5	<0.5	<0.5	<0.5	<0.5	<0.5
7-Acetyl-1,1,3,4,4,6-hexamethyl-1,2,3,4-tetrahydro-naphthalene (AHTN)	<0.5	<0.5	<0.5	<0.5	<0.5	<0.5	<0.5	<0.5
PAHs, fossil fuel components, and combustion byproducts								
Anthracene	<0.5	<0.5	<0.5	<0.5	<0.5	<0.5	<0.5	<0.5
Anthraquinone	<0.5	<0.5	<0.5	<0.5	<0.5	<0.5	<0.5	<0.5
p-Cresol	<1.0[b]	<1.0	<1.0	<1.0	0.04[c]	0.02[c]	<1.0	<1.0
Fluoranthene	<0.5	<0.5	<0.5	<0.5	<0.5	<0.5	<0.5	<0.5
Naphthalene	<0.5	<0.5[b]	<0.5	<0.5	<0.5	<0.5	<0.5	<0.5
1-Methylnaphthalene	<0.5	<0.5	<0.5	<0.5	<0.5	<0.5	<0.5	<0.5
2-Methylnaphthalene	<0.5	<0.5	<0.5	<0.5	<0.5	<0.5	<0.5	<0.5
2,6-Dimethylnaphthalene	<0.5	<0.5	<0.5	<0.5	<0.5	<0.5	<0.5	<0.5
Phenanthrene	<0.5	<0.5	<0.5	<0.5	<0.5	<0.5	<0.5	<0.5
Pyrene	<0.5	<0.5	<0.5	<0.5	<0.5	<0.5	<0.5	<0.5
Benzo[*a*]pyrene	<0.5	<0.5	<0.5	<0.5	<0.5	<0.5	<0.5	<0.5

Table 18. Concentrations of selected organic wastewater compounds in samples of water at various stages of treatment from municipal drinking-water treatment facilities in the Cape Fear River basin, North Carolina, July and August 2005.—Continued

[µg/L, microgram per liter; <, less than; PAH, polycyclic aromatic hydrocarbon; NA, not analyzed; analytes with known or suspected hormonal activity are shown in **bold** type; the method of analysis for data presented in this table corresponds to that described in Zaugg and others (2002)]

Site identifier (table 2; fig. 3)	CF-DW02			CF-DW06				
Treatment stage	Raw[a]	Raw[a]	Finished (chlorination)	Raw	Impounded	Settled	Clarified	Finished (chlorination)
Date sample collected	08/04/05			07/14/05				
Analyte (µg/L)								
Pesticides								
Bromacil	**<0.5**	**<0.5**	**<0.5**	**<0.5**	**<0.5**	**<0.5**	**<0.5**	**<0.5**
Carbaryl	**<1.0**	**<1.0**	**<1.0**	**<1.0**	**<1.0**	**<1.0**	**<1.0**	**<1.0**
Carbazole	<0.5	<0.5	<0.5	<0.5	<0.5	<0.5	<0.5	<0.5
Chlorpyrifos	**<0.5**	**<0.5**	**<0.5**	**<0.5**	**<0.5**	**<0.5**	**<0.5**	**<0.5**
Diazinon	**<0.5**	**<0.5**	**<0.5**	**<0.5**	**<0.5**	**<0.5**	**<0.5**	**<0.5**
d-Limonene	<0.5	<0.5	<0.5	<0.5	<0.5	<0.5	<0.5	<0.5
Metalaxyl	<0.5	<0.5	<0.5	<0.5	<0.5	<0.5	<0.5	<0.5
Metolachlor	<0.5	<0.5	<0.5	0.03[c]	0.04[c]	0.03[c]	0.03[c]	0.04[c]
Pentachlorophenol	**<2.0**	**<2.0**	**<2.0**	**<2.0**	NA	NA	**<2.0**	NA
Prometon	<0.5	<0.5	<0.5	<0.5	<0.5	<0.5	<0.5	<0.5
Pharmaceuticals and metabolites								
Caffeine[d]	0.04[c]	<0.5	<0.5	0.1[c]	0.05[c]	0.09[c]	0.08[c]	<0.5[b]
Cotinine[d]	<1.0	<1.0	<1.0	<1.0	<1.0	<1.0	<1.0	<1.0
Isoquinoline	<0.5	<0.5	<0.5	<0.5	<0.5	<0.5	<0.5	<0.5
Plasticizers								
Bisphenol A	**<1.0**	**<1.0**	**<1.0**	**<1.0**	NA	NA	**<1.0**	NA
Camphor	<0.5	<0.5	<0.5	<0.5	<0.5	<0.5[b]	<0.5	<0.5
Triethyl citrate (ethyl citrate)	<0.5	<0.5	<0.5	<0.5	<0.5	<0.5	<0.5	<0.5
Tri(2-butoxyethyl) phosphate	<0.5	<0.5	<0.5	<0.5	<0.5	<0.5	<0.5	<0.5
Solvents								
Isophorone	0.009[c]	<0.5	<0.5	0.01[c]	<0.5	<0.5	<0.5	<0.5[b]
Isopropylbenzene (cumene)	<0.5	<0.5	<0.5	<0.5	<0.5	<0.5	<0.5	<0.5
Tetrachloroethylene (PCE)	<0.5	<0.5	0.04[c]	<0.5	<0.5	<0.5	<0.5	0.03[c]
Biogenic sterols								
Cholesterol	<2.0	<2.0	<2.0	0.7[c]	<2.0	<2.0	<2.0[b]	<2.0
3-β-Coprostanol	<2.0	<2.0	<2.0	<2.0	<2.0	<2.0	<2.0	<2.0
β-Sitosterol	**<2.0**	**<2.0**	**<2.0**	**<2.0**	**<2.0**	**<2.0**	**<2.0**	**<2.0**
β-Stigmastanol	<2.0	<2.0	<2.0	<2.0	<2.0	<2.0	<2.0	<2.0
Miscellaneous compounds and dissolved organic carbon								
3-*t*-Butyl-4-hydroxyanisole (BHA)	**<5.0**	**<5.0**	**<5.0**	**<5.0**	**<5.0**	**<5.0**	**<5.0**	**<5.0**
1,4-Dichlorobenzene	**<0.5**	**<0.5**	**<0.5**	**<0.5**	**<0.5**	**<0.5**	**<0.5**	**<0.5**
5-Methyl-1H-benzotriazole	<2.0	<2.0	<2.0	<2.0	NA	NA	<2.0	NA
Bromoform	<0.5	0.08[c]	0.08[c]	<0.5	<0.5	0.41[c]	0.70[c]	1.6[c]
Triclosan	**<1.0**	**<1.0**	**<1.0**	**<1.0**	**<1.0**	**<1.0**	**<1.0**	**<1.0**
Dissolved organic carbon[e]	2,900	NA	19	2,100	930	110	76	7.7

Table 18. Concentrations of selected organic wastewater compounds in samples of water at various stages of treatment from municipal drinking-water treatment facilities in the Cape Fear River basin, North Carolina, July and August 2005.—Continued

[μg/L, microgram per liter; <, less than; PAH, polycyclic aromatic hydrocarbon; NA, not analyzed; analytes with known or suspected hormonal activity are shown in **bold** type; the method of analysis for data presented in this table corresponds to that described in Zaugg and others (2002)]

Site identifier (table 2; fig. 3)	CF-DW07					
Treatment stage	Raw[a]	Raw[a]	Preozonation	Settled	Clarified and ozonation (prefiltration)	Finished (chlorination)
Date sample collected			07/21/05			
Analyte (µg/L)						
Detergent components and degradates						
4-Cumylphenol	<1.0	<1.0	<1.0	<1.0	<1.0	<1.0
***p*-Nonylphenol (total)**	<5.0	<5.0	<5.0	<5.0	<5.0	<5.0
Nonylphenol diethoxylates (NP2EO)	<5.0	<5.0	<5.0	<5.0	<5.0	<5.0
4-*n*-Octylphenol	<1.0	<1.0	<1.0	<1.0	<1.0	<1.0
4-*t*-Octylphenol	<1.0	<1.0	<1.0	<1.0	<1.0	<1.0
4-*t*-Octylphenol monoethoxylates (OP1EO)	<1.0	<1.0	<1.0	<1.0	<1.0	<1.0
4-*t*-Octylphenol diethoxylates (OP2EO)	<1.0[b]	<1.0[b]	<1.0	<1.0	<1.0	<1.0
Flame retardants						
Tributyl phosphate	<0.5	<0.5	<0.5	<0.5	<0.5	<0.5
Tri(2-chloroethyl) phosphate	0.3[c]	0.4[c]	0.4[c]	0.3[c]	<0.5[b]	<0.5[b]
Tri(dichloroisopropyl) phosphate	<0.5[b]	<0.5[b]	<0.5[b]	<0.5[b]	<0.5[b]	<0.5[b]
Triphenyl phosphate	<0.5	<0.5	<0.5	<0.5	<0.5	<0.5
Fragrances						
Acetophenone	<0.5	<0.5	<0.5	<0.5	<0.5	<0.5
Benzophenone	<0.5	<0.5	<0.5	<0.5	<0.5	<0.5
1,3,4,6,7,8-Hexahydro-4,6,6,7,8,8-hexamethyl-cyclopenta-γ-2-benzopyran (HHCB)	<0.5	<0.5	<0.5	<0.5	<0.5	<0.5
Indole	<0.5	<0.5	<0.5	<0.5	<0.5	<0.5
3-Methyl-1H-indole (skatole)	<1.0	<1.0	<1.0	<1.0	<1.0	<1.0
Isoborneol	<0.5	<0.5	<0.5	<0.5	<0.5	<0.5
Menthol	<0.5	<0.5	<0.5	<0.5	<0.5	<0.5
Methyl salicylate	<0.5	<0.5	<0.5	<0.5	<0.5	<0.5
7-Acetyl-1,1,3,4,4,6-hexamethyl-1,2,3,4-tetrahydro-naphthalene (AHTN)	<0.5	<0.5	<0.5	<0.5	<0.5	<0.5
PAHs, fossil fuel components, and combustion byproducts						
Anthracene	<0.5	<0.5	<0.5	<0.5	<0.5	<0.5
Anthraquinone	<0.5	<0.5	<0.5	<0.5	<0.5	<0.5
p-Cresol	<1.0	<1.0	<1.0	<1.0	<1.0	<1.0
Fluoranthene	<0.5	<0.5	<0.5	<0.5	<0.5	<0.5
Naphthalene	<0.5	<0.5	<0.5	<0.5	<0.5	<0.5
1-Methylnaphthalene	<0.5	<0.5	<0.5	<0.5	<0.5	<0.5
2-Methylnaphthalene	<0.5	<0.5	<0.5	<0.5	<0.5	<0.5
2,6-Dimethylnaphthalene	<0.5	<0.5	<0.5	<0.5	<0.5	<0.5
Phenanthrene	<0.5	<0.5	<0.5	<0.5	<0.5	<0.5

Table 18. Concentrations of selected organic wastewater compounds in samples of water at various stages of treatment from municipal drinking-water treatment facilities in the Cape Fear River basin, North Carolina, July and August 2005.—Continued

[µg/L, microgram per liter; <, less than; PAH, polycyclic aromatic hydrocarbon; NA, not analyzed; analytes with known or suspected hormonal activity are shown in **bold** type; the method of analysis for data presented in this table corresponds to that described in Zaugg and others (2002)]

| Site identifier (table 2; fig. 3) | CF-DW07 | | | | | |
| Date sample collected | 07/21/05 | | | | | |
Treatment stage / Analyte (µg/L)	Raw[a]	Raw[a]	Preozonation	Settled	Clarified and ozonation (prefiltration)	Finished (chlorination)
Pyrene	<0.5	<0.5	<0.5	<0.5	<0.5	<0.5
Benzo[a]pyrene	<0.5	<0.5	<0.5	<0.5	<0.5	<0.5
Pesticides						
Bromacil	<0.5	<0.5	<0.5	<0.5	<0.5	<0.5
Carbaryl	<1.0	<1.0	<1.0	<1.0	<1.0	<1.0
Carbazole	<0.5	<0.5	<0.5	<0.5	<0.5	<0.5
Chlorpyrifos	<0.5	<0.5	<0.5	<0.5	<0.5	<0.5
Diazinon	<0.5	<0.5	<0.5	<0.5	<0.5[b]	<0.5
d-Limonene	<0.5	<0.5	<0.5	<0.5	<0.5	<0.5
Metalaxyl	<0.5	<0.5	<0.5	<0.5	<0.5	<0.5
Metolachlor	0.04[c]	0.04[c]	0.03[c]	<0.5	<0.5	<0.5
Pentachlorophenol	<2.0	<2.0	<2.0	<2.0	<2.0	<2.0
Prometon	<0.5	<0.5	<0.5	<0.5	<0.5	<0.5
Pharmaceuticals and metabolites						
Caffeine[d]	<0.5	<0.5	<0.5	<0.5	<0.5	<0.5[b]
Cotinine[d]	0.03[c]	0.03[c]	0.03[c]	0.03[c]	<1.0	<1.0
Isoquinoline	<0.5	<0.5	<0.5	<0.5	<0.5	<0.5
Plasticizers						
Bisphenol A	<1.0	<1.0	<1.0	<1.0	<1.0	<1.0
Camphor	<0.5	<0.5	<0.5	<0.5	<0.5	<0.5
Triethyl citrate (ethyl citrate)	<0.5	<0.5	<0.5	<0.5	<0.5	<0.5
Tri(2-butoxyethyl) phosphate	<0.5	<0.5	<0.5	<0.5	<0.5	<0.5
Solvents						
Isophorone	<0.5	<0.5	<0.5	<0.5	<0.5	<0.5
Isopropylbenzene (cumene)	<0.5	<0.5	<0.5	<0.5	<0.5	<0.5
Tetrachloroethylene (PCE)	<0.5	<0.5	<0.5	<0.5	<0.5	<0.5
Biogenic sterols						
Cholesterol	<2.0	<2.0	<2.0	<2.0	<2.0	<2.0
3-β-coprostanol	<2.0	<2.0	<2.0	<2.0	<2.0	<2.0
β-Sitosterol	<2.0	<2.0	<2.0	<2.0	<2.0	<2.0
β-Stigmastanol	<2.0	<2.0	<2.0	<2.0	<2.0	<2.0

Table 18. Concentrations of selected organic wastewater compounds in samples of water at various stages of treatment from municipal drinking-water treatment facilities in the Cape Fear River basin, North Carolina, July and August 2005.—Continued

[µg/L, microgram per liter; <, less than; PAH, polycyclic aromatic hydrocarbon; NA, not analyzed; analytes with known or suspected hormonal activity are shown in **bold** type; the method of analysis for data presented in this table corresponds to that described in Zaugg and others (2002)]

Site identifier (table 2; fig. 3)	CF-DW07					
Treatment stage	Raw[a]	Raw[a]	Preozonation	Settled	Clarified and ozonation (prefiltration)	Finished (chlorination)
Date sample collected			07/21/05			
Analyte (µg/L)						
Miscellaneous compounds and dissolved organic carbon						
3-*t***-Butyl-4-hydroxyanisole (BHA)**	<5.0	<5.0	<5.0	<5.0	<5.0	<5.0
1,4-Dichlorobenzene	<0.5	<0.5	<0.5	<0.5	<0.5	<0.5
5-Methyl-1H-benzotriazole	<2.0	<2.0	<2.0	<2.0	<2.0	<2.0
Bromoform	0.01[c]	0.009[c]	0.03[c]	0.03[c]	1.8[c]	3.8[c]
Triclosan	<1.0	<1.0	<1.0	<1.0	<1.0	<1.0
Dissolved organic carbon[e]	1,100	NA	540	68	10	7.3

[a] Replicate samples.

[b] Analyte detected in sample at a concentration less than 10 times that in an associated laboratory or field blank.

[c] Estimated concentration (analyte detected at a concentration outside the range of calibration).

[d] Secondary method of analysis for this analyte (see table 16 for preferred method of analysis).

[e] Concentration of dissolved organic carbon expressed in milligrams per liter.

Table 19. Concentrations of selected antibiotics, antibiotic metabolites, and pharmaceutical compounds in water at various stages of treatment from municipal drinking-water treatment facilities in the Tar River basin, North Carolina, February and June 2005.

[µg/L, microgram per liter; <, less than; the method of analysis for data presented in this table corresponds to that described in Meyer and others (2007)]

Site identifier (table 2; fig. 2)	Tar-DW02			Tar-DW03					
Treatment stage	Raw	Settled	Finished	Raw	Impounded	Settled	Filtered	Clarified	Finished
Date sample collected	02/11/05			06/24/05					
Analyte (µg/L)									
Macrolide antibiotic and metabolites									
Azithromycin[a]	0.011	<0.005	<0.005	<0.005	<0.005	0.005	<0.005	<0.005	<0.005
Erythromycin[a]	<0.005	<0.005	<0.005	<0.005	<0.005	<0.005	<0.005	<0.005	<0.005
Erythromycin-H_2O[b]	<0.005	<0.005	<0.005	<0.005	<0.005	<0.005	<0.005	<0.005	<0.005
Roxithromycin	<0.005	<0.005	<0.005	<0.005	<0.005	<0.005	<0.005	<0.005	<0.005
Tylosin	<0.005	<0.005	<0.005	<0.005	<0.005	<0.005	<0.005	<0.005	<0.005
Virginiamycin	<0.005	<0.005	<0.005	<0.005	<0.005	<0.005	<0.005	<0.005	<0.005
Fluoroquinolone antibiotics									
Ciprofloxacin	<0.005	<0.005	<0.005	<0.005	<0.005	0.005	<0.005	<0.005	<0.005
Enrofloxacin	<0.005	<0.005	<0.005	<0.005	<0.005	<0.005	<0.005	<0.005	<0.005
Lomefloxacin	<0.005	<0.005	<0.005	<0.005	<0.005	<0.005	<0.005	<0.005	<0.005
Norfloxacin	<0.005	<0.005	<0.005	<0.005	<0.005	<0.005	<0.005	<0.005	<0.005
Ofloxacin	<0.005	<0.005	<0.005	<0.005	<0.005	<0.005	<0.005	<0.005	<0.005
Sarafloxacin	<0.005	<0.005	<0.005	<0.005	<0.005	<0.005	<0.005	<0.005	<0.005
Sulfonamide antibiotics									
Sulfachloropyridazine	<0.005	<0.005	<0.005	<0.005	<0.005	<0.005	<0.005	<0.005	<0.005
Sulfadiazine	<0.005	<0.005	<0.005	<0.005	<0.005	<0.005	<0.005	<0.005	<0.005
Sulfadimethoxine	<0.005	<0.005	<0.005	<0.005	<0.005	<0.005	<0.005	<0.005	<0.005
Sulfamethazine	<0.005	<0.005	<0.005	<0.005	<0.005	<0.005	<0.005	<0.005	<0.005
Sulfamethoxazole[a]	<0.005	<0.005	<0.005	<0.005	<0.005	<0.005	<0.005	<0.005	<0.005
Sulfathiazole	<0.020	<0.020	<0.020	<0.020	<0.020	<0.020	<0.020	<0.020	<0.020
Tetracycline antibiotics and metabolites									
Chlortetracycline	<0.010	<0.010	<0.010	<0.010	<0.010	<0.010	<0.010	<0.010	<0.010
Iso-chlortetracycline[b]	<0.010	<0.010	<0.010	<0.010	<0.010	<0.010	<0.010	<0.010	<0.010
Epi-chlortetracycline[b]	<0.010	<0.010	<0.010	<0.010	<0.010	<0.010	<0.010	<0.010	<0.010
Epi-iso-chlortetracycline[b]	<0.010	<0.010	<0.010	<0.010	<0.010	<0.010	<0.010	<0.010	<0.010
Doxycycline	<0.010	<0.010	<0.010	<0.010	<0.010	<0.010	<0.010	<0.010	<0.010
Oxytetracycline	<0.010	<0.010	<0.010	<0.010	<0.010	<0.010	<0.010	<0.010	<0.010
Epi-oxytetracycline[b]	<0.010	<0.010	<0.010	<0.010	<0.010	<0.010	<0.010	<0.010	<0.010
Tetracycline	<0.010	<0.010	<0.010	<0.010	<0.010	<0.010	<0.010	<0.010	<0.010
Epi-tetracycline[b]	<0.010	<0.010	<0.010	<0.010	<0.010	<0.010	<0.010	<0.010	<0.010
Miscellaneous antibiotics									
Lincomycin	<0.005	<0.005	<0.005	<0.005	<0.005	<0.005	<0.005	<0.005	<0.005
Chloramphenicol	<0.010	<0.010	<0.010	<0.010	<0.010	<0.010	<0.010	<0.010	<0.010
Ormetoprim	<0.005	<0.005	<0.005	<0.005	<0.005	<0.005	<0.005	<0.005	<0.005
Trimethoprim[a]	<0.005	<0.005	<0.005	<0.005	<0.005	<0.005	<0.005	<0.005	<0.005
Pharmaceutical compounds									
Ibuprofen[a]	<0.050	<0.050	<0.050	<0.050	<0.050	<0.050	<0.050	<0.050	<0.050
Carbamazepine[a]	<0.005	<0.005	<0.005	0.008	<0.005	<0.005	<0.005	<0.005	<0.005

[a] Preferred method of analysis for this analyte (see table 15 for secondary method of analysis).

[b] Antibiotic metabolite.

Table 20. Concentrations of selected antibiotics, antibiotic metabolites, and pharmaceutical compounds in water at various stages of treatment from municipal drinking-water treatment facilities in the Cape Fear River basin, North Carolina, February and June 2005.

[μg/L, microgram per liter;<, less than; the method of analysis for data presented in this table corresponds to that described in Meyer and others (2007)]

Site identifier (table 2; fig. 3)	CF-DW02		CF-DW06				
Date sample collected	08/04/05		07/14/05				
Treatment stage	Raw	Finished (chlorination)	Raw	Impounded	Settled	Clarified	Finished (chlorination)
Analyte (μg/L)							
Macrolide antibiotics and metabolites							
Azithromycin[a]	<0.005	<0.005	<0.005	<0.005	<0.005	<0.005	<0.005
Erythromycin[a]	<0.008	<0.008	<0.005	<0.005	<0.005	<0.005	<0.005
Erythromycin-H_2O[b]	<0.008	<0.008	<0.005	<0.005	<0.005	<0.005	<0.005
Roxithromycin	<0.005	<0.005	<0.005	<0.005	<0.005	<0.005	<0.005
Tylosin	<0.005	<0.005	<0.005	<0.005	<0.005	<0.005	<0.005
Virginiamycin	<0.005	<0.005	<0.005	<0.005	<0.005	<0.005	<0.005
Fluoroquinoline antibiotics							
Ciprofloxacin	<0.005	<0.005	<0.005	<0.005	<0.005	<0.005	<0.005
Enrofloxacin	<0.005	<0.005	<0.005	<0.005	<0.005	<0.005	<0.005
Lomefloxacin	<0.005	<0.005	<0.005	<0.005	<0.005	<0.005	<0.005
Norfloxacin	<0.005	<0.005	<0.005	<0.005	<0.005	<0.005	<0.005
Ofloxacin	<0.005	<0.005	<0.005	<0.005	<0.005	<0.005	<0.005
Sarafloxacin	<0.005	<0.005	<0.005	<0.005	<0.005	<0.005	<0.005
Sulfonamide antibiotics							
Sulfachloropyridazine	<0.005	<0.005	<0.005	<0.005	<0.005	<0.005	<0.005
Sulfadiazine	<0.050	<0.050	<0.005	<0.005	<0.005	<0.005	<0.005
Sulfadimethoxine	<0.005	<0.005	<0.005	<0.005	<0.005	<0.005	<0.005
Sulfamethoxazole[a]	<0.005	<0.005	<0.005	<0.005	<0.005	<0.005	<0.005
Sulfamethazine	<0.005	<0.005	<0.005	<0.005	<0.005	<0.005	<0.005
Suflathiazole	<0.020	<0.020	<0.020	<0.020	<0.020	<0.020	<0.020
Tetracycline antibiotics and metabolites							
Chlortetracyline	<0.010	<0.010	<0.010	<0.010	<0.010	<0.010	<0.010
Epi-chlortetracycline[b]	<0.010	<0.010	<0.010	<0.010	<0.010	<0.010	<0.010
Epi-iso-chlortetracycline[b]	<0.010	<0.010	<0.010	<0.010	<0.010	<0.010	<0.010
Iso-chlortetracycline[b]	<0.010	<0.010	<0.010	<0.010	<0.010	<0.010	<0.010
Doxycycline	<0.010	<0.010	<0.010	<0.010	<0.010	<0.010	<0.010
Oxytetracycline	<0.010	<0.010	<0.010	<0.010	<0.010	<0.010	<0.010
Epi-oxytetracycline[b]	<0.010	<0.010	<0.010	<0.010	<0.010	<0.010	<0.010
Tetracycline	<0.010	<0.010	<0.010	<0.010	<0.010	<0.010	<0.010
Epi-tetracycline[b]	<0.010	<0.010	<0.010	<0.010	<0.010	<0.010	<0.010
Miscellaneous antibiotics							
Lincomycin	<0.005	<0.005	<0.005	<0.005	<0.005	<0.005	<0.005
Chloramphenicol	<0.010	<0.010	<0.010	<0.010	<0.010	<0.010	<0.010
Ormetoprim	<0.005	<0.005	<0.005	<0.005	<0.005	<0.005	<0.005
Trimethoprim[a]	<0.005	<0.005	<0.005	<0.005	<0.005	<0.005	<0.005
Pharmaceutical compounds							
Carbamazepine[a]	<0.005	0.006	0.008	0.015	0.008	0.006	0.006
Ibuprofen[a]	<0.050	<0.050	<0.050	<0.050	<0.050	<0.050	<0.050

Table 20. Concentrations of selected antibiotics, pharmaceutical compounds, and metabolites in water at various stages of treatment from municipal drinking-water treatment facilities in the Cape Fear River basin, North Carolina, February and June 2005.—Continued

[µg/L, microgram per liter;<, less than; the method of analysis for data presented in this table corresponds to that described in Meyer and others (2007)]

Site identifier (table 2; fig. 3)	CF-DW07				
Date sample collected	07/21/05				
Treatment stage	Raw	Preozonation	Settled	Clarification and ozonation (prefiltration)	Finished (chlorination)
Analyte (µg/L)					
Macrolide antibiotics and metabolites					
Azithromycin[a]	<0.005	<0.005	<0.005	<0.005	<0.005
Erythromycin[a]	<0.005	<0.005	<0.005	<0.005	<0.005
Erythromycin-H_2O[b]	<0.005	<0.005	<0.005	<0.005	<0.005
Roxithromycin	<0.005	<0.005	<0.005	<0.005	<0.005
Tylosin	<0.005	<0.005	<0.005	<0.005	<0.005
Virginiamycin	<0.005	<0.005	<0.005	<0.005	<0.005
Fluoroquinoline antibiotics					
Ciprofloxacin	<0.005	<0.005	<0.005	<0.005	<0.005
Enrofloxacin	<0.005	<0.005	<0.005	<0.005	<0.005
Lomefloxacin	<0.005	<0.005	<0.005	<0.005	<0.005
Norfloxacin	<0.005	<0.005	<0.005	<0.005	<0.005
Ofloxacin	<0.005	<0.005	<0.005	<0.005	<0.005
Sarafloxacin	<0.005	<0.005	<0.005	<0.005	<0.005
Sulfonamide antibiotics					
Sulfachloropyridazine	<0.005	<0.005	<0.005	<0.005	<0.005
Sulfadiazine	<0.005	<0.005	<0.005	<0.005	<0.005
Sulfadimethoxine	<0.005	<0.005	<0.005	<0.005	<0.005
Sulfamethoxazole[a]	<0.005	<0.005	<0.005	<0.005	<0.005
Sulfamethazine	<0.005	<0.005	<0.005	<0.005	<0.005
Suflathiazole	<0.020	<0.020	<0.020	<0.020	<0.020
Tetracycline antibiotics and metabolites					
Chlortetracyline	<0.010	<0.010	<0.010	<0.010	<0.010
Epi-chlortetracycline[b]	<0.010	<0.010	<0.010	<0.010	<0.010
Epi-iso-chlortetracycline[b]	<0.010	<0.010	<0.010	<0.010	<0.010
Iso-chlortetracycline[b]	<0.010	<0.010	<0.010	<0.010	<0.010
Doxycycline	<0.010	<0.010	<0.010	<0.010	<0.010
Oxytetracycline	<0.010	<0.010	<0.010	<0.010	<0.010
Epi-oxytetracycline[b]	<0.010	<0.010	<0.010	<0.010	<0.010
Tetracycline	<0.010	<0.010	<0.010	<0.010	<0.010
Epi-tetracycline[b]	<0.010	<0.010	<0.010	<0.010	<0.010
Miscellaneous antibiotics					
Lincomycin	<0.005	<0.005	<0.005	<0.005	<0.005
Chloramphenicol	<0.010	<0.010	<0.010	<0.010	<0.010
Ormetoprim	<0.005	<0.005	<0.005	<0.005	<0.005
Trimethoprim[a]	<0.005	<0.005	<0.005	<0.005	<0.005
Pharmaceutical compounds					
Carbamazepine[a]	0.006	0.005	<0.005	<0.005	<0.005
Ibuprofen[a]	<0.050	<0.050	<0.050	<0.050	<0.050

[a] Preferred method of analysis for this analyte (see table 16 for secondary method of analysis).

[b] Antibiotic metabolite.

The most commonly detected OWCs were HHCB and the flame retardants tri(dichloroisopropyl) phosphate and tri(2-chloroethyl) phosphate, which were detected in all effluent samples (table 13). Other commonly detected OWCs included 1,4-dichlorobenzene and benzophenone detected in seven samples; and AHTN, *p*-cresol, and triethyl citrate, which were detected in six samples. The herbicide, metolachlor, was detected in effluent from all WWTPs except site Tar-WW01 (table 13), whereas prometon, also a herbicide, was only detected in effluent samples from site Tar-WW01 (table 13). The pesticide, pentachlorophenol, was detected only in samples from site Tar-WW03 (table 13), and carbaryl, another pesticide, was detected only in effluent samples from sites Tar-WW03 and CF-WW07. Caffeine (based on secondary method) was detected in effluent samples from all WWTPs except site CF-WW07. Similarly, plasticizers were detected in effluent samples from all facilities except CF-WW07. Bisphenol A, a plasticizer with demonstrated hormonal activity, was detected in effluent from Tar-WW01 at concentrations ranging from 0.2 to 0.3 µg/L (table 13). The plasticizers triethyl citrate and tri(2-butoxyethyl) phosphate also were detected in effluent samples (table 13).

Among the antibiotics analyzed during phase 2 of the study, ciprofloxacin, ofloxacin, azithromycin, and trimethoprim were detected in all effluent samples (table 14). Carbamazepine, an antiepileptic drug, also was detected in all effluent samples analyzed with the preferred method. Sulfamethoxazole and erythromycin (including its metabolite erythromycin-H_2O) also were detected in most effluent samples (table 14). Similarities in the measured concentrations of analytes in samples of wastewater effluent collected before and after disinfection (by either chlorination or UV irradiation) indicated that disinfection had little effect on most compounds.

Drinking-Water Samples at Various Stages of Treatment

Most of the OWCs, pharmaceutical compounds, and antibiotics detected in raw drinking-water samples were not detected in the treated drinking water (tables 15–20). Diphenhydramine was the only pharmaceutical compound detected in finished water samples from DWTPs in the Tar River basin (table 15), whereas cotinine and carbamazepine (secondary method) were the only pharmaceutical compounds detected in finished water samples from DWTPs in the Cape Fear River basin (table 16). Diphenhydramine was detected at a concentration of 0.012 µg/L in the finished water sample from site Tar-DW03 (table 15). Cotinine concentrations in finished water samples from DWTPs in the Cape Fear River basin ranged from 0.009 µg/L at site CF-DW02 to 0.004 µg/L at site CF-DW07. Carbamazepine (secondary method) was detected at a concentration of 0.009 µg/L in finished water from site CF-DW02. Regulatory standards have not been established for diphenhydramine, cotinine, or carbamazepine.

Concentrations of OWCs in drinking-water samples are listed in tables 17 and 18 for DWTPs in the Tar and Cape Fear River basins, respectively. Bromoform, a disinfection byproduct, was the only analyte detected at concentrations that exceeded water-quality criteria. Bromoform was detected in all finished water samples with concentrations ranging from 0.04 to 26 µg/L. The highest concentration of bromoform was in finished water from the Tarboro DWTP (26 µg/L) and exceeded the North Carolina water-quality criterion of 4.3 µg/L; however, this concentration is less than the U.S. Environmental Protection Agency (USEPA) Maximum Contaminant Level (MCL) of 80 µg/L for total trihalo-methanes (U.S. Environmental Protection Agency, 2006; table 4). Flame retardants were the most commonly detected OWCs in water samples from DWTPs and were detected more commonly in samples from the Cape Fear River basin than from the Tar River basin. The herbicide, metolachlor, was detected in finished water from site CF-DW06 at an estimated concentration of 0.04 µg/L. This concentration is much lower than the USEPA Lifetime Health Advisory for metolachlor of 700 µg/L (table 4). Pesticides were not detected in finished water samples from any of the other sites. The solvent, tetrachloroethylene, was detected in finished water samples from sites Tar-DW03, CF-DW02, and the CF-DW06 at estimated concentrations ranging from 0.02 to 0.04 µg/L, which are more than 100 times less than the MCL of 5 µg/L (U.S. Environmental Protection Agency, 2006; table 4).

Antibiotics were rarely detected in raw drinking-water samples and were not detected in any of the finished water samples from DWTPs in the Tar and Cape Fear River basins (tables 19 and 20, respectively). Azithromycin was detected only in the raw drinking-water sample from site Tar-DW02. The antiepileptic compound carbamazepine, however, was detected in finished water from site CF-DW02 and site CF-DW06 at an estimated concentration of 0.006 µg/L. Drinking-water treatment processes resulted in removal of most analytes present in raw water samples. Several compounds—azithromycin, carbamazepine, caffeine, and cotinine—seem to be recalcitrant to removal by drinking-water treatment processes.

Summary

Selected pharmaceutical compounds and metabolites and OWCs were detected in samples of municipal wastewater and raw and finished drinking water from treatment facilities in the Tar and Cape Fear River basins. Concentrations of most analytes were less than reporting limits. The only analyte that exceeded water-quality criteria was the disinfection byproduct, bromoform, which was detected at a concentration of 26 µg/L in a finished water sample from site Tar-DW02. Concentrations and the number of analytes detected were greater in samples from treated effluent than from raw drinking-water samples. Drinking-water treatment practices resulted in decreased concentrations of these analytes, with few compounds detected in finished water. Wastewater disinfection processes, chlorination and UV irradiation, seem to have little effect on the concentrations of these analytes. Because of the small number of samples analyzed during this study, the results may not be representative of water-quality conditions at various times of the year or during different streamflow conditions.

References Cited

Aherne, G.W., and Briggs, R., 1989, The relevance of the presence of certain synthetic steroids in the aquatic environment: Journal of Pharmacy and Pharmacology, v. 41, no. 10, p. 735–736.

Cahill, J.D., Furlong, E.T., Burkhardt, M.R., Kolpin, D., and Anderson, L.G., 2004, Determination of pharmaceutical compounds in surface- and ground-water samples by solid-phase extraction and high-performance liquid chromatography-electrospray ionization mass spectrometry: Journal of Chromatography, v. 1041, p. 171–180.

Clara, M., Strenn, B., and Kreuzinger, N., 2004, Carbamazepine as a possible anthropogenic marker in the aquatic environment: Investigations on the behaviour of carbamazepine in wastewater treatment and during groundwater infiltration: Water Research, v. 38, no. 4, p. 947–954.

Daughton, C.G., and Ternes, T.A., 1999, Pharmaceuticals and personal care products in the environment: Agents of subtle change?: Environmental Health Perspectives, v. 107, p. 907–938.

Falconer, I., Chapman, H.F., Moore, M.R., and Ranmuthugala, G., 2006, Endocrine-disrupting compounds: A review of their challenge to sustainable and safe water supply and water reuse: Environmental Toxicology, v. 21, no. 2, p. 181–191.

Fent, K., Weston, A.A., and Caminada, D., 2006, Ecotoxicology of human pharmaceuticals: Aquatic Toxicology, v. 76, p. 122–159.

Hirsch, R., Ternes, T., Haberer, K., and Kratz, K.L., 1999, Occurrence of antibiotics in the aquatic environment: Science of the Total Environment, v. 225, p. 109–118.

Jones, O.A.H., Voulvoulis, N., and Lester, J.N., 2004, Potential ecological and human health risks associated with the presence of pharmaceutically active compound in the aquatic environment: Critical Reviews in Environmental Science and Chemistry, v. 54, no. 4, p. 335–350.

Jones, O.A.H., Voulvoulis, N., and Lester, J.N., 2005, Human pharmaceuticals in wastewater treatment processes: Critical Reviews in Environmental Science and Chemistry, v. 55, p. 401–427.

Kolpin, D.W., Furlong, E.T., Meyer, M.T., Thurman, E.M., Zaugg, S.D., Barber, L.B., and Buxton, H.T., 2002, Pharmaceuticals, hormones, and other organic wastewater contaminants in U.S. streams, 1999–2000: A national reconnaissance: Environmental Science and Technology, v. 36, no. 6, p. 1202–1211.

Kolpin, D.W., Skopec, M., Meyer, M.T., Furlong, E.T., and Zaugg, S.D., 2004, Urban contribution of pharmaceuticals and other organic wastewater contaminants to streams during differing flow conditions: Science of the Total Environment, v. 328, p. 119–130.

Meyer, M.T., Lee, E.A., Ferrell, G.M., Bumgarner, J.E., and Varns, Jerry, 2007, Evaluation of offline tandem and online solid-phase extraction with liquid chromatography/electrospray ionization-mass spectrometry for analysis of antibiotics in ambient water and comparison to an independent method: U.S. Geological Survey Scientific Investigations Report 2007–5021, 28 p.

North Carolina Department of Environment and Natural Resources, Division of Water Quality, Planning Branch, 2004, Surface-water intakes, digital vector dataset one-map_prod.SDEADMIN.swi, distributed by North Carolina Center for Geographic Information and Analysis, Raleigh, NC; meta data accessed September 11, 2008, at http://www.nconemap.org/nconemap_meta/swi.xml

North Carolina Department of Environment and Natural Resources, Division of Water Quality, Planning Branch, 2006, National pollutant discharge elimination system sites, digital vector dataset Onemap_prod.SDEADMIN.npdes, distributed by North Carolina Center for Geographic Information and Analysis, Raleigh, NC; meta data accessed September 11, 2008, at http://www.nconemap.org/nconemap_meta/npdes.xml

North Carolina Department of Environment and Natural Resources, Division of Water Quality, 2008, North Carolina and Environmental Protection Agency criteria table; accessed August 15, 2008, at http://h2o.enr.state.nc.us/csu/documents/NC_EPA_Standards_CriteriaTables1-10-08.pdf

North Carolina Department of Environment and Natural Resources, Division of Water Resources, 2002, 2002 Local water supply plans; accessed September 11, 2008, at http://www.ncwater.org/Water_Supply_Planning/Local_Water_Supply_Plan/

Stackelberg, P., Furlong, E., Meyer, M., Zaugg, S., Henderson, A., and Reissman, D., 2004, Persistence of pharmaceutical compounds and other organic wastewater contaminants in a conventional drinking-water-treatment plant: Science of the Total Environment, v. 329, p. 99–113.

Stackelberg, P.E., Gibs, J., Furlong, E.T., Meyer, M.T., Zaugg, S.D., and Lippincott, R.L., 2007, Efficiency of conventional drinking-water-treatment processes in removal of pharmaceuticals and other organic compounds: Science of the Total Environment, v. 377, p. 255–272.

Ternes, T.A., Meisenheimer, M., McDowell, D., Sacher, F., Brauch, H.-J., Haist-Gulde, B., Preuss, G., Wilme, U., and Zulei-Seibert, N., 2002, Removal of pharmaceuticals during drinking water treatment: Environmental Science and Technology, v. 36, p. 3855–3863.

U.S. Environmental Protection Agency, 2006, 2006 Edition of the drinking water standards and health advisories: Washington, DC, U.S. Environmental Protection Agency, Office of Water, Report EPA 822-R-06-013; accessed September 11, 2008, at http://www.epa.gov/waterscience/criteria/drinking/dwstandards.pdf

Vieno, N., Tukhanen, T., and Kronberg, L., 2007, Elimination of pharmaceuticals in sewage treatment plants in Finland: Water Research, v. 41, p. 1001–1012.

Watkinson, A.J., Murby, E.J., and Costanzo, S.D., 2007, Removal of antibiotics in conventional and advanced wastewater treatment: Implications for environmental discharge and wastewater recycling: Water Research, v. 41, p. 4164–4176.

Wershaw, R.L., Fishman, M.J., Grabbe, R.R., and Lowe, L.E., eds., 1987, Methods for the determination of organic substances in water and fluvial sediments: U.S. Geological Survey Techniques of Water-Resources Investigations, book 5, chap. A3, 80 p.

Westerhoff, P., Yoon, Y., Snyder, S., and Wert, E., 2005, Fate of endocrine-disruptor, pharmaceutical, and personal care product chemicals during simulated drinking water treatment processes: Environmental Science and Technology, v. 39, p. 6649–6663.

Zaugg, S.D., and Leiker, T.J., 2006, Review of method performance and improvements for determining wastewater compounds (Schedule 1433), National Water Quality Laboratory Technical Memorandum 2006.01, dated May 3, 2006; accessed September 11, 2008, at http://nwql.usgs.gov/Public/tech_memos/nwql.2006-01 html

Zaugg, S.D., Smith, S.G., Schroeder, M.P., Barber, L.B., and Burkhardt, M.R., 2002, Methods of analysis by the U.S. Geological Survey National Water Quality Laboratory—Determination of wastewater compounds by polystyrene-divinylbenzene solid-phase extraction and capillary-column gas chromatography/mass spectrometry: U.S. Geological Survey Water-Resources Investigations Report 01–4186, 37 p.

Prepared by:
USGS Publishing Network
Raleigh Publishing Service Center
3916 Sunset Ridge Road
Raleigh, NC 27607

For additional information regarding this publication, contact:
Gloria M. Ferrell
U.S. Geological Survey
3916 Sunset Ridge Road
Raleigh, NC 27612
phone: 919-571-4057
email: gferrell@usgs.gov

Or visit the North Carolina Water Science Center Web site at:
http://nc.water.usgs.gov

Ferrell—Occurrence of Selected Pharmaceuticals and OWCs in Effluent and Water Samples from the Tar and Cape Fear River Basins—Open-File Report 2009-1046

Printed on recycled paper